Roadmap to Retirement

Bill Ilgenfritz
Ilgenfritz Financial Group – Senior Tax Solutions

Copyright © 2022 by Bill Ilgenfritz.

All rights reserved. No part of this publication may be reproduced, distributed, or transmitted in any form or by any means, including photocopying, recording, or other electronic or mechanical methods, without the prior written permission of the publisher, except in the case of brief quotations embodied in critical reviews and certain other noncommercial uses permitted by copyright law. For permission requests, write to the publisher at the address below. These materials are provided to you by Bill Ilgenfritz for informational purposes only and Bill Ilgenfritz and Advisors Excel, LLC expressly disclaim any and all liability arising out of or relating to your use of same. The provision of these materials does not constitute legal or investment advice and does not establish an attorney-client relationship between you and Bill Ilgenfritz. No tax advice is contained in these materials. You are solely responsible for ensuring the accuracy and completeness of all materials as well as the compliance, validity, and enforceability of all materials under any applicable law. The advice and strategies found within may not be suitable for every situation. You are expressly advised to consult with a qualified attorney or other professional in making any such determination and to determine your legal or financial needs. No warranty of any kind, implied, expressed, or statutory, including but not limited to the warranties of title and non-infringement of third-party rights, is given with respect to this publication.

Bill Ilgenfritz
Ilgenfritz Financial Group – Senior Tax Solutions

1603 Rodney Road
York, PA 17408

215 North Main Street
Shrewsbury, PA 17361

https://IFGFinancial.com

Book layout ©2020 Advisors Excel, LLC

Roadmap To Retirement/Bill Ilgenfritz.
First Edition

ISBN 979-8-414011-70-5
ISBN (hardcover): 978-1-956220-36-0

Printed in China

Bill Ilgenfritz is a licensed insurance agent in the states of Pennsylvania and Maryland. Ilgenfritz Financial Group – Senior Tax Solutions is an independent financial services firm that helps individuals create retirement strategies using a variety of insurance products to custom suit their needs and objectives.

The contents of this book are provided for informational purposes only and are not intended to serve as the basis for any financial decisions. Any investment, tax, legal, or estate planning information is general in nature. It should not be construed as investment, legal or tax advice. Always consult a financial advisor, attorney, or tax professional regarding the applicability of this information to your unique situation.

Information presented is believed to be factual and up-to-date, but we do not guarantee its accuracy, and it should not be regarded as a complete analysis of the subjects discussed. All expressions of opinion are those of the author as of the date of publication and are subject to change. Content should not be construed as personalized financial advice nor should it be interpreted as an offer to buy or sell any financial products mentioned. A qualified financial professional should be consulted before implementing any of the strategies presented.

Investing involves risk, including the potential loss of principal. Any references to protection benefits or guaranteed/lifetime income streams refer only to fixed insurance products, not securities or investment products. Insurance and annuity product guarantees are backed by the financial strength and claims-paying ability of the issuing insurance company. Bill Ilgenfritz is not licensed to provide products or advice related to the sales or liquidation of securities.

Any names used in the examples in this book are hypothetical only and do not represent actual clients.

"Winners never quit, and quitters never win."

~ Vince Lombardi

This book is dedicated to my grandparents, Bill and Sue Maugans, who inspired me to do bigger things and gave me a deep sense of purpose through their love for one another.

Table of Contents

The Importance of Planning 1
Longevity 7
Taxes 23
Market Volatility 29
Retirement Income 35
Social Security 49
401(k)s & IRAs 63
Annuities 73
Estate & Legacy 81
Long-Term Care Insurance 91
Finding a Financial Professional 99
Acknowledgments 107
About the Author 109

FOREWORD
The Importance of Planning

In the early 2000s, a gentleman brought his dog into our office. We found this peculiar, but we later learned that he was going to have to go home that evening and tell his wife he'd lost all of their money in the stock market. He didn't really want to go home, and he probably needed his dog for "moral support" on that dark day.

Greed often puts people into the stock market, and greed usually keeps them there longer than they should stay. This client had invested heavily in tech stocks (which were highly popular at the time), and when the tech "bubble" burst in 2000, he was not alone in having suffered substantial losses.

Stock investments can help you amass money ... but they don't constitute a true plan for creating a retirement income you can rely on—one you can't outlive, whether you're around until age seventy-eight or to 108.

At Ilgenfritz Financial Group, when we create a true income plan, we typically move at least a portion of a client's savings into annuities and other solid financial instruments that can provide them with a guaranteed income for life.

We plan for the expenses folks will have in retirement—both the obvious and the non-obvious. For instance, we know inflation isn't going away. Things are going to cost more in the future, and retirees will likely need more money than they currently spend to make ends meet.

Expenses are only going to get more expensive!

Planning for retirement expenses (both expected and unexpected) is only one way we help our clients in our role as retirement and financial planners. We'll sit down and look at *everything* the client has as they approach retirement. What will your Social Security or pension payments be? What is the status of your IRA, your 401(k), or 403(b)? These are the building blocks that will form your retirement income plan.

***

One thing folks should know is that we operate completely differently from the way a stockbroker does. Brokers usually want to keep the accumulation going, and they'll show a client high rates of return and investments they could use that might "beat the index." But that doesn't work as a way to guarantee *income* for retirees—income they can count on for the rest of their lives.

Instead of "pushing" any particular investment or financial products, our firm helps clients create a true *"Roadmap to Retirement"*—a solid plan that takes them all the way to and through their retirement with the income they'll need.

This is an approach in which we are strong believers. Why? It's no fun going to bed at night and worrying about whether you're going to have enough money. I can't say how many clients have come to our firm with that very concern: They're concerned about whether they can make ends meet in retirement.

A lot of that worry comes from having a good portion of your nest egg in investments like stocks, where you could make money—or lose it. That money isn't safe. We move that money out into instruments that will guarantee your income. One of the best tools we can use to do this is a *fixed index annuity*, which still allows your money to grow at a modest rate, but guarantees that you can't lose money.

***

Many clients aren't aware of some basic facts about retirement income. For instance, when one spouse passes away, the other spouse does not collect both Social Security checks. The surviving spouse only gets the larger of the two checks. They now have to live on less income, even though their household expenses will not have decreased as significantly as their income.

Some clients have made certain choices regarding their retirement savings plans (401(k), IRA, pension) which will mean that income could be significantly reduced (or vanish) at some point in the future.

And many clients aren't aware of the fixed indexed annuities that will likely be the key to their guaranteed income. If they've been working with a fee-based advisor or broker, that person would not make much money "selling" such products, so they often won't even mention them.

We recently had a client who had a significant nest egg, but they were paying about $13,000 per year in fees to have their money "managed." One reason is that when the market goes up, the "manager" makes even more money, but when things go poorly for the client's investments, the manager still collects a hefty fee. We were able to show the client a our approach to plan for their retirement—where we don't charge fees for "managing" your nest egg.

***

Our clients have dreams and aspirations, of course; we also have aspirations for them, which drives our zeal for helping folks retire the right way.

Ideally, our clients and their spouses will all live long, healthy lives. But of course, none of us live forever. Our passion is for helping retiring people and couples enjoy worry-free retirements, now and in the future, whether they're together, or finishing the journey on their own.

We want to make sure both spouses are aware of what choices have been made in the past regarding retirement savings. For instance, if the husband made elections that would mean his pension plans would end upon his death, regardless of whether the wife survives, we want to make sure the wife understands this so there are no unpleasant surprises.

Regardless of the choices that were made when your retirement instruments were established, one thing is almost universally true: In retirement, you're going to need more money than you think.

Here are some of the other topics we're always sure to cover with our retiring clients:

- When we talk about planning, we're going to be talking about tax planning, too, with their CPA or financial advisor. Many savings programs include deferred taxes: "an IOU to the IRS." That makes the IRS the retiree's biggest beneficiary! We seek ways to make their family members their bigger beneficiaries, rather than the IRS.
- We don't want our clients to go broke in a nursing home. Senior care facilities are extremely expensive today, and those expenses likely won't decrease. We've seen people exhaust their retirement—going completely broke, including having to sell their homes—due to hefty nursing home fees. And those are only going up.
- There are plans for the informed, and there are plans for the uninformed. The "plan" for the uninformed is not a plan at all ... it's the idea that you'll have to sell everything you have and give it all to a nursing home. We make plans for the informed: Our *Roadmap to Retirement* doesn't lead to going broke in a nursing home!
- Tax rates also are not likely to decrease in the future; they're only headed in one direction, and that's UP. Part of some recent tax reductions passed by the federal government included lower tax brackets for everyone. However, these tax breaks will "sunset" if Congress does nothing to extend them, at which points those rates will go back to where they were before, if not higher.
- The costs of everything from taxes to health care are likely to increase during your retirement, and that's why you need to be talk to a true retirement advisor, not a fee-based broker.

**

This is just a partial list of the many reasons you need a solid plan, backed by the kind of experience and expertise only a firm like ours can offer.

You need a true *Roadmap to Retirement*.

CHAPTER 1

Longevity

You would think the prospect of the grave would loom more frightening as we age, yet many retirees say their number one fear is actually running out of money in their twilight years.[1] This fear is, unfortunately, justified, in part, because of one significant factor: We're living longer.

According to the Social Security Administration, in 1950, the average life expectancy for a sixty-five-year-old man was seventy-eight, and the average for a sixty-five-year-old woman was eighty-one. In 2020, those averages were eighty-three and eighty-eight, respectively.[2]

The bottom line of many retirees' budget woes comes down to this: They just didn't plan to live so long. Now, when we are younger and in our working years, that's not something we necessarily see as a bad thing; don't some people fantasize about living forever or, at least, reaching the ripe old age of one hundred?

However, with a longer lifespan, as we near retirement, we face a few snags. Our resources are finite—we only have so

---

[1] Liz Weston. nerdwallet.com. March 25, 2021. "Will You Really Run Out of Money in Retirement?"
https://www.nerdwallet.com/article/finance/will-you-really-run-out-of-money-in-retirement

[2] Social Security Administration. 2011 Trustees Report. "Actuarial Publications: Cohort Life Expectancy."
https://www.ssa.gov/OACT/TR/2011/lr5a4.html

much money to provide income—but our lifespans can be unpredictably long, perhaps longer than our resources allow. Also, longer lives don't necessarily equate with healthier lives. The longer you live, the more money you will likely need to spend on health care, even excluding long-term care needs like nursing homes.

You will also run into inflation. If you don't plan to live another twenty-five years but end up doing so, inflation at an average 3 percent will approximately double the price of goods over that time period. Put a harsh twist on that and the buying power of a ninety-year-old will be half of what they possessed if they retired at sixty-five.[3] And this is before you count the expenses of any potential health care or long-term care needs.

Because we don't necessarily get to have our cake and eat it, too, our collective increased longevity hasn't necessarily increased the healthy years of our lives. Typically, our life-extending care most widely applies to the time in our lives where we will need more care in general. Think of common situations like a pacemaker at eighty-five, or cancer treatment at seventy-eight.

"Wow, Bill," I can hear you say. "Way to start with the good news first."

I know, I've painted a grim picture. But all I'm concerned about here is the cost. It's hard to put a dollar sign on life, but that is essentially what we're talking about when discussing longevity and your finances. According to the Stanford Center on Longevity, more than half of pre-retirees underestimate the life expectancy of the average sixty-five-year-old.[4] Living longer isn't a bad thing; it just costs more, and one key to a sound retirement strategy is preparing in advance for that expense.

---

[3] Bob Sullivan, Benjamin Curry. Forbes. April 28, 2021. "Inflation And Retirement Investments: What You Need to Know."
https://www.forbes.com/advisor/retirement/inflation-retirement-investments/

[4] Stanford Center on Longevity. "Underestimating Years in Retirement."
http://longevity.stanford.edu/underestimating-years-in-retirement/

One client of mine, "Mary," did a lot of things just right. She had a pension plan, and saved a great deal of money as well. She's now ninety-eight years old, and thanks to her *Roadmap*, she still has just about all the money with which she started retirement! She's one example of a client who really planned for income in retirement ... she's living a long and robust life, and she planned for it!

We have another client who's 108! And she still has to file a tax return every year.

One of our clients had this advice on retirement communities and senior care facilities: "Too many people move in too late, when their needs are dire." She moved in during her sixties, and she feels she got a lot more "bang for her buck." She's now ninety-eight, and has been enjoying the fellowship of other seniors—people with similar interests and tastes—for many years.

Another example: One woman I know illustrates this picture perfectly. Her mother passed away in her late seventies after years of suffering from Alzheimer's disease. Her father died at eighty from cancer. With modern medicine and treatment, this woman survived two rounds of breast cancer, lived with diabetes, and relied on a pacemaker, extending her life to age eighty-eight, nearly a decade beyond what she anticipated. However, she and her husband had saved and planned for "just in case," trying to be prepared if they had to move, needed nursing home care, or needed to help children and grandchildren with their expenses. One of their "just-in-case" scenarios was living much longer than they anticipated. The last six years of her life were fraught with medical expenses, but she was also blessed with knowing her five great-grandchildren and deepening relationships with her children and grandchildren. She was able to pay for her own medical care, including her final two years in a nursing home, and her twilight years were truly golden.

From age eighty-five to eighty-eight, she was more socially active, with many visits from family and friends. She participated in more activities than she had in the seven years since her husband died. Her planning from decades earlier allowed her to pass on a legacy to her children when she passed away herself. The legacy she left behind can be measured both in dollar signs *and* in other intangible ways.

Living longer may be more expensive, but it can be so meaningful when you plan for your "just-in-cases."

Retiring Later

Planning for a long life in retirement partly depends on when you retire. While many people end up retiring earlier than they anticipated—due to injuries, layoffs, family crises, and other unforeseen circumstances—continuing to work past age sixty (and even sixty-five) is still a viable option for others and can be an excellent way to help establish financial comfort in retirement.

There are many reasons for this. For one, you obviously still earn a paycheck and the benefits accompanying it. Medical coverage and beefing up your retirement accounts with further savings can be significant by themselves but continuing your income also should keep you from dipping into your retirement funds, further allowing them the opportunity to grow.

Additionally, for many workers, their nine-to-five job is more than just clocking in and out. Having a sense of purpose can keep us active physically, mentally, and socially. That kind of activity and level of engagement may also help stave off many of the health problems that plague retirees. Avoiding a sedentary life is one of the advantages of staying plugged into the workforce, if possible.

We had a client who retired early, and then spent a lot of his money: He needed motorcycles and other toys! Soon, though, he ran through his retirement savings, and had to go back to work. He's now driving a bus.

Many of our clients are still working in their mid-seventies for far better reasons: They enjoy the fulfillment their careers give them. Several have told us they wouldn't want to retire: "I wouldn't know what to do with myself!" Getting up and going to work every day is one of the great ways a person can feel a sense of purpose.

Health Care

Take a second to reflect on your health care plan. Although working up to or even past age sixty-five would allow you to avoid a coverage gap between your working years and Medicare, that may not be an option for you. Even if it is, when you retire, you will need to make some decisions about what kind of insurance coverage you may need to supplement your Medicare. Are there any medical needs you have that may require coverage in addition to Medicare? Did your parents or grandparents have any inherited medical conditions you might consider using a special savings plan to cover?

These are all questions that are important to review with your financial professional so you can be sure you have enough money put aside for health care.

Long-Term Care

Longevity means the need for long-term care is statistically more likely to happen. If you intend to pass on a legacy, planning for long-term care is paramount, since most estimates project nearly 70 percent of Americans will need some type of it.[5] However, this may be one of the biggest, most stressful pieces of longevity preparation I encounter in my work. For one thing, who wants to talk about the point in their lives when they may feel the most limited? Who wants to dwell

---

[5] LongTermCare.gov. February 18, 2020. "How Much Care Will You Need?" https://acl.gov/ltc/basic-needs/how-much-care-will-you-need

on what will happen if they no longer can toilet, bathe, dress, or feed themselves?

I get it; this is a less-than-fun part of the process. But a little bit of preparation now can go a long way!

When it comes to your longevity, just like with your goals, one of the important things to do is sit and dream. It may not be the fun, road-trip-to-the-Grand-Canyon kind of dreaming, but you can spend time envisioning how you want your twilight years to look.

For instance, if it is important for you to live in your home for as long as possible, who will provide for the day-to-day fixes and to-dos of housework if you become ill? Will you set aside money for a service, or do you have relatives or friends nearby whom you could comfortably allow to help you? Do you prefer in-home care over a nursing home or assisted living? This could be a good time to discuss the possibility of moving into a retirement community versus staying where you are or whether it's worth moving to another state and leaving relatives behind.

These are all important factors to discuss with your spouse and children, as *now* is the right time to address questions and concerns. For instance, is aging in place more important to one spouse than the other? Are the friends or relatives who live nearby emotionally, physically, and financially capable of helping you for a time if you face an illness?

Many families I meet with find these conversations very uncomfortable, particularly when children discuss nursing home care with their parents. A knee-jerk reaction for many is to promise they will care for their aging parents. This is noble and well-intentioned, but there needs to be an element of realism here. Does "help" from an adult child mean they stop by and help you with laundry, cooking, home maintenance, and bills? Or does it mean they move you into their spare room when you have hip surgery? Are they prepared to help you use the restroom and bathe if that becomes difficult for you to do on your own?

I don't mean to discourage families from caring for their own; this can be a profoundly admirable relationship when it works out. However, I've seen families put off planning for late-in-life care based on a tenuous promise that the adult children would care for their parents, only to watch as the support system crumbles. Sometimes this is because the assumed caregiver hasn't given serious thought to the preparation they would need, both in a formal sense and regarding their personal physical, emotional, and financial commitments. This is often also because we can't see the future: Alzheimer's disease and other maladies of old age can exact a heavy toll. When a loved one reaches the point where he or she is at risk of wandering away or needs help with two or more activities of daily living, it can be more than one person or family can realistically handle.

If you know what you want, communicate with your family about both the best-case and worst-case scenarios. Then, hope for the best, and plan for the worst.

Realistic Cost of Care

Wrapped up in your planning should be a consideration for the cost of long-term care. One study estimates that by 2030, the nation's long-term care costs could reach $2.5 trillion as roughly 24 million Americans require some type of long-term care.[6] The potential costs for such care and treatment can be underestimated, especially by those who have maintained robust health and find it difficult to envision future declines to their condition.

Another piece of preparing for long-term care costs is anticipating inflation. It's common knowledge that prices have been and keep rising, and that will lower your purchasing

---

[6] Tara O'Neill Hayes, Sara Kurtovic. Americanactionforum.org. February 18, 2020. "The Ballooning Costs of Long-Term Care."
https://www.americanactionforum.org/research/the-ballooning-costs-of-long-term-care/

power on everything from food to medical care. Long-term care is a big piece of the inflation-disparity pie, which is part of why many find their estimates of nursing home care widely miss the mark. According to one survey, people expected to pay around $25,350 in out-of-pocket long-term care expenses per year, but, in reality, they'll more likely be paying over $47,000.[7]

While local costs vary from state to state, here's the national median for various forms of long-term care (plus projections that account for a 3 percent annual inflation, so you can see what I'm talking about):[8]

	Long-Term Care Costs: Inflation			
	Home Health Care, Homemaker Services	Adult Day Care	Assisted Living	Nursing Home (semi-private room)
Annual 2021	$59,484	$20,280	$54,000	$94,896
Annual 2031	$79,944	$27,252	$72,576	$127,536
Annual 2041	$107,436	$36,624	$97,536	$171,396
Annual 2051	$144,384	$49,224	$131,076	$230,340

---

[7] Moll Law Group. 2021. "The Cost of Long-Term Care." https://www.molllawgroup.com/the-cost-of-long-term-care.html
[8] Genworth Financial. January 31, 2022. "Cost of Care Survey 2021." https://www.genworth.com/aging-and-you/finances/cost-of-care.html

Fund Your Long-Term Care

One critical mistake I see are those who haven't planned for long-term care because they assume the government will provide everything. But that's a big misconception. The government has two health insurance programs: Medicare and Medicaid. These can greatly assist you in your health care needs in retirement but usually don't provide enough coverage to cover all your health care costs in retirement. My firm isn't a government outpost, so we don't get to make decisions when it comes to forming policy and specifics about either one of these programs. I'm going to give the overview of both, but if you want to dive into the details of these programs, you can visit www.Medicare.gov and www.Medicaid.gov.

Medicare

Medicare covers those aged sixty-five and older and those who are disabled. Medicare's coverage of any nursing-home-related health issues is limited. It might cover your nursing home stay if it is not a "custodial" stay, and it isn't long-term. For example, if you break a bone or suffer a stroke, stay in a nursing home for rehabilitative care, and then return home, Medicare may cover you. But, if you have developed dementia or are looking to move to a nursing facility because you can no longer bathe, dress, toilet, feed yourself, or take care of your hygiene, etc., then Medicare is not going to pay for your nursing home costs.[9]

Medicaid

Medicaid is a program the states administer, so funding, protocol, and limitations vary. Compared to Medicare, Medicaid more widely covers nursing home care, but it targets a different demographic than Medicare: those with low incomes.

---

[9] Medicare.gov. "What Part A covers." https://www.medicare.gov/what-medicare-covers/part-a/what-part-a-covers.html

If you have more assets than the Medicaid limit in your state and need nursing home care, you will need to use those assets to pay for your care. You will also have a list of additional state-approved ways to spend some of these assets over the Medicaid limit, such as pre-purchasing burial plots and funeral expenses or paying off debts. After that, your remaining assets fund your nursing home stay until they are gone, at which point Medicaid will jump in.

Some people aren't stymied by this, thinking they will just pass on their financial assets early, gifting them to relatives, friends, and causes so they can qualify for Medicaid when they need it. However, to prevent this exact scenario, Uncle Sam has implemented the look-back period. Currently, if you enroll in Medicaid, you are subject to having the government scrutinize the last five years of your finances for large gifts or expenses that may subject you to penalties, temporarily making you ineligible for Medicaid coverage.

So, if you're planning to preserve your money for future generations and retain control of your financial resources during your lifetime, you'll probably want to prepare for the costs of longevity beyond a "government plan."

Self-Funding

One way to fund a longer life is the old-fashioned way, through self-funding. There are a variety of financial tools you can use, and they all have their pros and cons. If your assets are in low-interest financial vehicles (savings, bonds, CDs), you risk letting inflation erode the value of your dollar. Or, if you are relying on the stock market, you have more growth potential, but you'll also want to consider the possible implications of market volatility. What if your assets take a hit? If you suffer a loss in your retirement portfolio in early or mid-retirement, you might have the option to "tighten your belt," so to speak, and cut back on discretionary spending to allow your portfolio the room to bounce back. But, if you are retired and depend on income from a stock account that just hit a downward stride, what are you going to do?

HSAs

These days, you might also be able to self-fund through a health savings account, or HSA, if you have access to one through a high-deductible health plan (you will not qualify to save in an HSA after enrolling in Medicare). In an HSA, any growth of your tax-deductible contributions will be tax-free, and any distributions paid out for qualified health costs are also tax-free. Long-term care expenses count as health costs, so, if this is an option available to you, it is one way to use the tax advantages to self-fund your longevity. Bear in mind, if you are younger than sixty-five, any money you use for nonqualified expenses will be subject to taxes and penalties, and, if you are older than sixty-five, any HSA money you use for non-medical expenses is subject to income tax.

LTCI

One slightly more nuanced way to pay for longevity, specifically for long-term care, is long-term care insurance, or LTCI. As car insurance protects your assets in case of a car accident and home insurance protects your assets in case something happens to your house, long-term care insurance aims to protect your assets in case you need long-term care in an at-home or nursing home situation.

As with other types of insurance, you will pay a monthly or annual premium in exchange for an insurance company paying for long-term care down the road. Typically, policies cover two to three years of care, which is adequate for an "average" situation: it's estimated 70 percent of Americans will need about three years of long-term care of some kind. However, it's important to consider you might not be "average" when you are preparing for long-term care costs; on average, 20 percent of today's sixty-five-year-olds could need care for longer than five years.[10]

---

[10] LongTermCare.gov. February 18, 2020. "How Much Care Will You Need?" https://acl.gov/ltc/basic-needs/how-much-care-will-you-need

Now, there are a few oft-cited components of LTCI that make it unattractive for some:

- Expense — LTCI can be expensive. It is generally less expensive the younger you are, but a fifty-five-year-old couple who purchased LTCI in 2020 could expect to pay $2,080 each year for an average three-year coverage policy. And the annual cost only increases from there the older you are.[11]
- Limited options — Let's face it: LTCI may be expensive for consumers, but it can also be expensive for companies that offer it. With fewer companies willing to take on that expense, this narrows the market, meaning opportunities to price shop for policies with different options or custom benefits are limited.
- If you know you need it, you might not be able to get it — Insurance companies offering LTCI are taking on a risk that you may need LTCI. That risk is the foundation of the product—you may or may not need it. If you know you will need it because you have a dementia diagnosis or another illness for which you will need long-term care, you will likely not qualify for LTCI coverage.
- Use it or lose it—If you have LTCI and are in the minority of Americans who die having never needed long-term care, all the money you paid into your LTCI policy is gone.
- Possibly fluctuating rates—Your rate is not locked in on LTCI. Companies maintain the ability to raise or lower your premium amounts. This means some seniors face an ultimatum: Keep funding a policy at what might be a less affordable rate *or* lose coverage and let go of all the money they paid in so far.

---

[11] American Association for Long-Term Care Insurance. January 12, 2021. "2021 National Long-Term Care Insurance Price Index." https://www.aaltci.org/news/long-term-care-insurance-association-news/2021-long-term-care-insurance-price-index-released-for-age-55

After that, you might be thinking, "How can people possibly be interested in LTCI?" But let me repeat myself—as many as 70 percent of Americans will need long-term care. And, although only 8 percent of Americans have purchased LTCI, keep in mind the high cost of nursing home care. Can you afford $7,000 a month to put into nursing home care and still have enough left over to protect your legacy? This is a very real concern: One study says 72 percent of Americans are impoverished by the end of just one year in a nursing home.[12] So, not to sound like a broken record, but it is vitally important to have a plan in place to deal with longevity and long-term care if you intend to leave a financial legacy.

We offer asset-based LTCI, which means the client is going to take some money (typically $50-100,000) and turn that into a lump sum to cover long-term care. One of our clients is an electrical engineer in his sixties, and he's already been diagnosed with early-onset Alzheimer's disease. For people like this, an investment in LTCI provides confidence they'll be taken care of financially. And when the client passes away, an LTCI plan can include a death benefit, which will go to the spouse.

People who bought LTCI in the past (1980s to early 2000s) often had plans that required them to pay monthly premiums. What those products didn't take into consideration was the rising costs of care, such that some insured clients have been told they need to pony up more money if they want the same benefits, or keep the same premiums and see their benefits reduced from what they thought they'd be getting.

One of my clients who bought LTCI years ago paid $26,000, and was told that would be the extent of her LTCI benefit. How long do you think $26,000 would last, given today's health care costs? Unfortunately, not very long.

---

[12] A Place for Mom. January 2018. "Long-Term Care Insurance: Costs & Benefits." http://www.aplaceformom.com/senior-care-resources/articles/long-term-care-costs.

Product Riders

LTCI and self-funding are not the only ways to plan for the expenses of longevity. Some companies are getting creative with their products, particularly insurance companies. One way they are retooling to meet people's needs is through optional product riders on annuities and life insurance. Elsewhere in this book, I talk about annuity basics, but here's a brief overview: Annuities are insurance contracts. You pay the insurance company a premium, either as a lump sum or as a series of payments over a set amount of time, in exchange for guaranteed income payments. One of the advantages of an annuity is it has access to riders, which allow you to tweak your contract for a fee, usually about 1 percent of the contract value annually. One annuity rider some companies offer is a long-term care rider. If you have an annuity with a long-term care rider and are not in need of long-term care, your contract behaves as any annuity contract would—nothing changes. Generally speaking, if you reach a point when you can't perform multiple functions of daily life on your own, you notify the insurance company, and a representative will turn on those provisions of your contract.

Like LTCI, different companies and products offer different options. Some annuity long-term care riders offer coverage of two years in a nursing home situation. Others cap expenses at two times the original annuity's value. It greatly depends. Some people prefer this option because there isn't a "use-it-or-lose-it" piece; if you die without ever having needed long-term care, you still will have had the income benefit from the base contract. Still, as with any annuities or insurance contracts, there are the usual restrictions and limitations. Withdrawing money from the contract will affect future income payments, early distributions can result in a penalty, income taxes may apply, and, because the insurance company's solvency is what guarantees your payments, it's important to do your research about the insurance company you are considering purchasing a contract from.

Understandably, a discussion on long-term care is bound to feel at least a little tedious. Yet, this is a critical piece of preparing for income in retirement, particularly if you want to leave a legacy.

Eighty-four percent of people don't have any long-term care plan. Some have to sell off assets to pay for it, and that often leaves their surviving spouse in "spousal poverty." When I do dinner presentations, and I ask for a show of hands from people who have planned for their long-term care, I typically see very few raised hands, yet about 70 percent of retirees are going to need long-term care of some kind.[13] It's time to plan for the future.

Spousal Planning

Here's one thing to keep in mind no matter how you plan to save: Many of us will be planning for more than ourselves. Look back at all the stats on health events and the likelihood of long life and long-term care. If they hold true for a single individual, then the likelihood of having a costly health or long-term care event is even higher for a married couple. You'll be planning for not just one life, but two. So, when it comes to long-term care insurance, annuities, self-funding, or whatever strategy you are looking at using, be sure you are funding longevity for the both of you.

Many people do it right. Some move into facilities earlier than they absolutely have to, and end up not having to use much of their LTCI.

---

[13] Kate Dore. CNBC. Aug. 26, 2021. "Most retirees will need long-term care. These are the best ways to pay for it."
https://www.cnbc.com/2021/08/26/most-retirees-will-need-long-term-care-these-are-ways-to-pay-for-it-.html

CHAPTER 2

Taxes

Where to begin with taxes? Perhaps by acknowledging we all bear responsibility for the resources we share. Roads, bridges, schools ... It is the patriotic duty of every American to pay their fair share of taxes. Many would agree with me, though, while they don't mind paying their fair share, they're not interested in paying one cent more than that!

Now, just talking taxes probably takes your mind to April—tax season. You are probably thinking about all the forms you collect and how you file. Perhaps you are thinking about your certified public accountant or another qualified tax professional and saying to yourself, "I've already got taxes taken care of, thanks!"

However, what I see when people come into my office is that their relationship with their tax professional is purely a January through April relationship. That means they may have a tax professional, but not a tax *planner*.

What I mean is tax planning extends beyond filing taxes. In April, we are required to settle our accounts with the IRS to make sure we have paid up on our bill or to even the score if we have overpaid. But real tax planning is about making each financial move in a way that allows you to keep the most money in your pocket and out of Uncle Sam's.

Now, as a caveat, I want to emphasize I am neither a CPA nor a tax planner, but I see the way taxes affect my clients, and I have plenty of experience helping clients implement tax-efficient strategies in their retirement income plans using various insurance and annuity products in conjunction with their tax professionals.

Our firm offers in-house tax services for our senior clients, in that we show them ways to keep more of their hard-earned dollars in their pocket. We show them ways to keep more of their Social Security protected from taxation. The IRS is not obligated to share any tax reduction strategies, but it's my job to share these strategies with our clients.

It is especially important to me to help my clients develop tax-efficient strategies in their retirement income strategies because each dollar they can keep in their pockets is a dollar we can put to work.

We had a client who came in for tax services because of our competitively priced returns. He was using a CPA previously and I asked him if he liked paying taxes. As with most clients, of course, his answer was "no." He asked if his CPA did something wrong, and I said he hadn't done "wrong"—he simply didn't tell you how to pay less in taxes. After we made some changes to his tax return, we were able to save him $4,100 a year. That's $340 more in his pocket every month.

The Fed

Now, in the United States, taxes can be a rather uncertain proposition. Depending on who is in the White House and which party controls Congress, we might be tempted to assume tax rates could either decline or increase in the next four to eight years accordingly. However, there is one (large!) factor we, as a nation, must confront: the national debt.

Currently, according to USDebtClock.org, we are over $26,500,000,000,000 in debt and climbing. That's $26.5 *trillion* with a "T." With just $1 trillion, you could park it in the bank at a zero percent interest rate and still spend more than $54 million every day for fifty years without hitting a zero balance.

Even if Congress got a handle and stopped that debt from its daily compound, divided by each taxpayer, we each would owe about $214,000. So, will that be check or cash?

My point here isn't to give you anxiety. I'm just saying, even with the rosiest of outlooks on our personal income tax rates, none of us should count on low tax rates for the long term. Instead, you and your network of professionals (tax, legal, and financial) should constantly be looking for ways to take advantage of tax-saving opportunities as they come. After all, the best "luck" is when proper planning meets opportunity.

So, how can we get started?

Know Your Limits

One of the foundational pieces of tax planning is knowing what tax bracket you are in, based on your income after subtracting pre-tax or untaxed assets. Your income taxes are based on your taxable income.

One reason to know your taxable income and your income tax rate is so you can see how far away you are from the next lower or higher tax bracket. This is particularly important when it comes to decisions such as gifting and Roth IRA rollovers. You will want to be sure to talk to a tax professional and a financial advisor registered to provide investment advice before making any decisions.

For instance, based on the 2020 tax table, Mallory and Ralph's taxable income is just over $330,000, putting them in the 32 percent tax bracket and about $3,400 above the upper end of the 24 percent tax bracket. They have already maxed out their retirement funds' tax-exempt contributions for the year. Their daughter, Gloria, is a sophomore in college. This couple could shave a considerable amount off their tax bill if they use the $3,400 to help Gloria out with groceries and school—something they were likely to do, anyway, but now can deliberately be put to work for them in their overall financial strategy.

Now, I use Mallory and Ralph only as an example—your circumstances are probably different—but I think this nicely illustrates the way planning ahead for taxes can save you money.

Assuming a Lower Tax Rate

Many people anticipate being in a lower tax bracket in retirement. It makes sense: You won't be contributing to retirement funds; you'll be drawing from them. And you won't have all those work expenses—work clothes, transportation, etc.

Yet, do you really plan on changing your lifestyle after retirement? Do you plan to cut down on the number of times you eat out, scale back vacations, and skimp on travel?

What I see in my office is many couples spend more in the first few years, or maybe the first decade, of retirement. Sure, that may taper off later on, but usually only just in time for their budget to be hit with greater health and long-term care expenses. Do you see where this is going? Many people plan as though their taxable income will be lower in retirement and are surprised when the tax bills come in and look more or less the same as they used to. It's better to plan for the worst and hope for the best, wouldn't you agree?

401(k)/IRA

One sometimes-unexpected piece of tax planning in retirement concerns your 401(k) or IRA. Most of us have one of these accounts or an equivalent. Throughout our working lives, we pay in, dutifully socking away a portion of our earnings in these tax-deferred accounts. There's the rub: tax-deferred. Not tax-free. Very rarely is anything free of taxation when you get down to it. Using 401(k)s and IRAs in retirement is no different. The taxes the government deferred when you were in your working years are now coming due, and you will pay taxes on all the money you withdraw from those accounts at whatever your current tax rate is.

Just to ensure Uncle Sam gets his due, the government also has a required minimum distribution, or RMD, rule. Beginning at age seventy-two, you are required to withdraw a certain minimum amount every year from your 401(k) or IRA, or else you will face a 50 percent tax penalty on any RMD monies you should have withdrawn but didn't—and that's on top of income tax.

Of course, there is also the Roth account. You can think of the difference between a Roth and a traditional retirement account as the difference between taxing the seed and taxing the harvest. Because Roths are funded with post-tax dollars, there aren't tax penalties for early withdrawals of the principal nor are there taxes on the growth after you reach age fifty-nine-and-one-half. Perhaps best of all, there are no RMDs. Of course, you must own a Roth account for a minimum of five years before you are able to take advantage of all its features.

This is one more area where it pays to be aware of your tax bracket. Some people may find it advantageous to "convert" their traditional retirement account funds to Roth account funds in a year during which they are in a lower tax bracket. Others may opt to put any excess RMDs from their traditional retirement accounts into other products, like stocks or insurance.

Does that make your head spin? Understandable. That's why it's so important to work with a financial professional and tax planner who can help you not only execute these sorts of tax-efficient strategies but also help you understand what you are doing and why.

We had been talking to several clients about taxation and retirement, and we brought to their attention the impact higher taxes can have in the later years. What many people don't know when saving money in a 401(k) or 403(b) plan is that at some point, you are going to need to pay tax on all those dollars. We believe taxes are only going up after the COVID-19 pandemic. We don't know how big the coming increases will be, but we do know that if Congress does nothing, the Sunset Provision of the Tax Code will increase tax brackets substantially. Some people with a half-million dollar account could pay as much as $580,000 in taxes over their lifetime through required minimum distributions, and as a "death tax" when your children inherit your money.

CHAPTER 3

Market Volatility

Up and down. Roller coaster. Merry-go-round. Bulls and bears. Peak-to-trough.
Sound familiar? This is the language we use to talk about the stock market. With volatility and spikes, even our language is jarring, bracing, and vivid.

Still, financial strategies tend to revolve around market-based products because there is no other financial class that packs the same potential for growth, pound for pound, as stock-based products.

However, along with the potential for growth is the potential for loss. Many of the people I see in my office come in still feeling a bit burned from the market drama of 2000 to 2010. That was a rough stretch.

So how do we balance these factors? How do we try to satisfy both the need for protection and the need for growth?

For one thing, it is important to recognize the value of diversity. Now, I'm not just talking about the diversity of assets among different kinds of stocks, or even different kinds of stocks and bonds. That's only one kind of diversity; both stocks and bonds, though different, are still market-based products. Most market-based products, even within a diverse portfolio, tend to rise or lower as a whole, just like an incoming tide. Therefore, a portfolio diverse in only market-sourced products won't automatically protect your assets during times when the market declines.

In addition to the sort of "horizontal diversity" you have by purchasing a variety of stocks and bonds from different companies, I encourage having "vertical diversity," or diversity among asset classes. This means having different product types with varying levels of growth potential, liquidity, and protection—all in accordance with your unique situation, goals, and needs. This will often involve the assistance of a securities-registered individual who can offer you investment products for your portfolio, when needed.

Many financial advisors talk about the Rule of 100. The Rule of 100 states that as you get older, the portion of your account allocated to stocks should decrease, and the proportion allocated to bonds should increase. It's called the Rule of 100 because the theory is that you should subtract your age from 100, and that's the percentage of your portfolio you should have in the stock market; as your age goes up, your stock market exposure goes down. The intent of the Rule of 100 is to help you get more conservative with your retirement accounts later in life.

But even with this rule, you can still have losses. For most of my clients, when I ask them how much they can afford to lose, they tell me they don't want to lose *any* money! So we put them in products that guarantee they cannot lose money due to market volatility. With these products, under the worst-case scenario, the client's portfolio would get zero growth in a year when the market went negative.

The Color of Money

When you're looking at the overall diversity of your portfolio, part of the equation is knowing which products fit in what category: what has liquidity, what has protection, and what has growth potential.

Before we dive in, keep in mind these aren't absolutes. You might think of liquidity, growth, and protection as primary colors. While some products will look pretty much yellow, red, or blue, others will have a mix of characteristics, making them more green, orange, or purple.

Growth

I like to think of the growth category as red. It's powerful, it's somewhat volatile, and it's also the category where we have the greatest opportunities for growth and loss. Often, products in the growth category will have a good deal of liquidity but very little protection. These are our market-based products and strategies, and we think of them mostly in shades of red and orange, to designate their growth and liquidity. This is a good place to be when you're young—think fast cars and flashy leather jackets—but its allure often wanes as you move closer to retirement. Examples of "red" products include:
- Stocks
- Equities
- Exchange-traded funds
- Mutual funds
- Corporate bonds
- Real estate investment trusts
- Speculations
- Alternative investments

Liquidity

Yellow is my liquid category color. I typically recommend having at least enough yellow money to cover six months' to a year's worth of expenses in case of emergency. Yellow assets don't need a lot of growth potential; they just need to be readily available when we need them. The "yellow" category includes:
- Cash
- Money market accounts

Protection

The color of protection, to me, is blue. Tranquil, peaceful, sure, even if it lacks a certain amount of flash. This is the direction I like to see people generally move toward as they're nearing retirement. The red, flashy look of stock market returns and the risk of possible overnight losses is less attractive as we near retirement and look for more consistency and reliability. While this category doesn't come with a lot of liquidity, the products here are backed by an insurance company, a bank, or a government entity. "Blue" products include:

- Certificates of deposit (backed by banks)
- Government-based bonds (backed by the U.S. government)
- Life insurance (backed by insurance companies)
- Annuities (backed by insurance companies)

All funds carry some level of risk. With mutual funds, you might lose some or all of the money you invested because the securities held by the fund can go down in value. Dividends or interest payments may also change as market conditions change. The more volatile the funds, the higher the investment risk.

With stocks, companies that have been around for 100 years have gone under (companies like Remington Arms and Brooks Brothers), while companies you'd never think would survive have (General Motors, for example—which did file Chapter 11 bankruptcy, and would have gone under but for a government bailout).[14]

---

[14] Barbara Farfan. March 12, 2019. The Balance. "General Motors Chapter 11 Bankruptcy in the US." https://www.thebalancesmb.com/gm-chapter-11-2891901

Dollar-Cost Averaging

With 401(k)s and other market-based retirement products (IRAs, 403(b)s, etc.), when you are investing for the long term, dollar-cost averaging is a concept that can work in your favor. When the market is trending up, if you are consistently paying in money, month over month, great; your investments can grow, and you are adding to your assets. When the market takes a dip, no problem; your dollars buy more shares at a lower price. At some point, we hope the market will rebound, in which case your shares can grow and possibly be more valuable than they were before. This concept is what we call dollar-cost averaging. While it can't ensure a profit or guarantee against losses, it's a time-tested strategy for investing in a volatile market.

However, when you are in retirement, this strategy may work against you. You may have heard of "reverse" dollar-cost averaging. Before, when the market lost ground, you were "bargain-shopping"; your dollars purchased more assets at a reduced price. When you are in retirement, you are no longer the purchaser; you are selling. So, in a down market, you have to sell more assets to make the same amount of money as what you made in a favorable market.

I've had lots of people step into my office saying, "My advisor says the market always bounces back, and I have to just hold on for the long term."

There's a basis for this thinking; thus far, the market has always rebounded to higher heights than before. But this is no guarantee, and the prospect of potentially higher returns in five years may not be very helpful in retirement if you are relying on the income from those returns to pay this month's electric bill, for example. That's why, at our firm, we specialize in insurance strategies that help provide a reliable stream of income.

When we meet with our clients, we talk about having a paycheck for the rest of their lives that they can never outlive. We find out what other sources of income they have: Pensions,

Social Security, or any other investments. We then look at insurance products with income riders that can guarantee that when they are ready to start taking distributions, they'll never outlive their stream of income.

Is There a "Perfect" Product?

To bring us back around to the discussion of protection, growth, and liquidity, the ideal product would be a "ten" in all three categories, right? Completely guaranteed, doubling in size every few years, and accessible whenever you want. Does such a product exist? Anyone who says, "yes" is either ignorant or malevolent.

Instead of running in circles looking for that perfect product, the silver bullet, the unicorn of financial strategies, it's more important to circle back to the concept of a balanced, asset-diverse retirement portfolio.

This is why your interests may be best served when you work with a team of qualified financial professionals who know what various financial products can do and how to use them in your personal retirement plan.

At Ilgenfritz Financial Group, we talk about equity indexed annuities that guarantee upside potential with no downside risk. When clients want to keep their hard-earned dollars, they cannot risk a market correction that could essentially wipe out a third to 50 percent of their retirement savings. With these types of products, your upside potential is limited, but you can't lose money—you simply get a "zero" in a year when the market goes negative. We believe all seniors agree that they can't lose money because they don't have the time to recover from their losses.

CHAPTER 4
Retirement Income

Retirement. For many of us, it's what we've saved for and dreamed of, pinning our hopes to a magical someday. Is that someday full of traveling? Is it filled with grandkids? Gardening? Maybe your fondest dream is simply never having to work again, never having to clock in or be accountable to someone else.

Your ability to do these things all hinges on *income*. Without the money to support these dreams, even a basic level of work-free lifestyle is unsustainable. That's why planning for your income in retirement is so foundational. But where do we begin?

It's easy to feel overwhelmed by this question. Some may feel the urge to amass a large lump sum and then try to put it all in one product—insurance, investments, liquid assets—to provide all the growth, liquidity, and income they need. Instead, I think you need a more balanced approach. After all, retirement planning isn't magic. There is no single product that can be all things to all people (or even all things to one person). No approach works unilaterally for everyone. That's why it's important to talk to a financial professional who can help you lay down the basics and take you step-by-step through the process. Not only will you have the assurance that you have addressed the areas you need to, but you will also have an ally who can help you break down the process and help keep you from feeling overwhelmed.

Sources of Income

Thinking of all the pieces of your retirement expenses might be intimidating. But, like cleaning out a junk drawer or revisiting that garage remodel, once you have laid everything out, you can begin to sort things into categories.

Once you have a good overall picture of where your expenses will lie, you can start stacking up the resources to cover them.

Social Security

Social Security is a guaranteed, inflation-protected federal insurance program playing a significant part in most of our retirement plans. From delaying until you've reached full retirement age or beyond to examining spousal benefits, as I discuss elsewhere in this book, there is plenty you can do to try to make the most of this monthly benefit. As with all your retirement income sources, it's important to consider how to make this resource stretch to provide the most bang and buck for your situation.

Pension

Another generally reliable source of retirement income for you might be a pension, if you are one of the lucky people who still has one.

If you don't have a pension, go ahead and skim on to the next section. If you do have a pension, keep on reading.

Because your pension can be such a central piece of your retirement income plan, you will want to put some thought into answering basic questions about it.

How well is your pension funded? Since the heyday of the pension plan, companies and governments have neglected to fund their pension obligations, causing a persistent problem with this otherwise reliable asset. Public pensions face a collective $4.998 trillion deficit, according to the U.S. Pension Tracker.[15] The Public Benefit Guaranty Association, which helps insure private pensions, reports that there is a $63.7 billion shortfall in multiemployer plans, affecting half of all multiemployer plans.[16] If you have a pension, it is quite possibly included in those statistics.

In addition to checking up on your pension's health, check into what your options are for withdrawing your pension. If you have already retired and made those decisions, this may be a foregone conclusion. If not, it pays to know what you can expect and what decisions you can make, such as taking spousal options to cover your husband or wife if he or she outlives you.

Also, some companies are incentivizing lump-sum payouts of pensions to reduce the companies' payment liabilities. If that's the case with your employer, talk to your financial professional to see if it might be prudent to do something like that or if it might be better to stick with lifetime payments or other options.

Your 401(k) and IRA

One "modern way" to save for retirement is in a 401(k) or IRA (or their nonprofit or governmental equivalents). These tax-advantaged accounts are, in my opinion, a poor substitute for pensions, but one of the biggest disservices we do to ourselves is to not take full advantage of them in the first place. According to one article, only 32 percent of Americans invest in a 401(k), though 59 percent of employed Americans have access to a 401(k) benefit option. [17]

---

[15] U.S. Pension Tracker. April 2021. us.pensiontracker.org
[16] Pension Benefit Guaranty Corporation. December 10, 2020. "Deficit FAQs." https://www.pbgc.gov/about/faq/pg/deficit-faqs
[17] Amin Dabit. personalcapital.com. April 1, 2021. "The Average 401k Balance by Age." https://www.personalcapital.com/blog/retirement-planning/average-401k-balance-age/

Also, if you have changed jobs over the years, do the work of tracking down any benefits from your past employers. You might have an IRA here or a 401(k) there; keep track of those so you can pull them together and look at those assets when you're ready to look at establishing sources of retirement income.

Do You Have...

- Life insurance?
- Annuities?
- Long-term care insurance?
- Any passive income sources?
- Stock and bond portfolios?
- Liquid assets? (What's in your bank account?)
- Alternative investments?
- Rental properties?

It's important, if you are going through the work of sitting with a financial professional, to look at your full retirement income picture and pull together *all* your assets, no matter how big or small. From the free insurance policy offered at your bank to the sizable investment in your brother-in-law's modestly successful furniture store, you want to have a good idea of where your money is.

I recently met with a client who came in to see me after he attended one of my seminars. He said he normally just puts his statements in a drawer and doesn't look at them. He was amazed to find out that his accounts have grown to $2.1 million and that he could have retired five years ago if he had looked at his statements and worked with an advisor like me. We put together an income strategy for him and his wife. Now, the couple will be able to enjoy their golden years no matter what life throws at them.

Retirement Income Needs

How much income will you need in retirement? How do you determine that? A lot of people work toward a random number, thinking, "If I can just have a million dollars, I'll be comfortable in retirement!" Don't get me wrong; it is possible to save up a lot of money and then retire in the hopes you can keep your monthly expenses lower than some set estimation. But I think this carries a general risk of running out of money. Instead, I work with my clients to find out what their current and projected income needs are and then work from there to see how we might cover any gaps between what they have and what they want.

Goals and Dreams

I like to start with your pie in the sky. Do you find yourself planning for your vacations more thoroughly than you do your retirement? It's not uncommon for Americans to spend more time planning our vacations than we spend planning our retirements. Maybe it's because planning a vacation is less stressful: Having a week at the beach go awry is, well, a walk on the beach compared to running out of money in retirement. Whatever the case, perhaps it would be better if you thought of your retirement as a vacation in and of itself—no clocking in, no boss, no overtime. If you felt unlimited by financial strain, what would you do?

Would an endless vacation for you mean Paris and Rome? Would it mean mentoring at children's clubs or serving at the local soup kitchen? Or maybe it would mean deepening your ties to those immediately around you—neighbors, friends, and family. Maybe it would mean more time to take part in the hobbies and activities you love. Have you been considering a second (or even third) act as a small-business owner, turning a hobby or passion into a revenue source?

This is your time to daydream and answer the question: If you could do anything, what would you do?

After that, it's a matter of putting a dollar amount on it. What are the costs of round-the-world travel? One couple I know said their highest priority in retirement was being able to take each of their grandchildren on a cross-country vacation every year. That's a pretty specific goal—one that is reasonably easy to nail down a budget for.

We have several clients who decided to sell their home, buy a motor home, and travel to see all that the United States has to offer. They visit national parks and monuments, and a few of them are still doing so to this day. They've always dreamed about traveling, and thought it would be neat to be able to stop as long as they wanted to and take in our country's beauty.

Current Budget

Compiling a current expense report can be one of the trickiest pieces of retirement preparation. Many people assume the expenses of their lives in retirement will be different—lower. After all, there will be no drive to work, no need for a formal wardrobe, and, perhaps most impactful of all, no more saving for retirement!

Yet, we often underestimate our daily spending habits. That's why I typically ask my clients to bring in their bank statements for the past year—they are reflective of your *actual* spending, not just what you think you're spending.

We look at a few things when determining a client's income needs. The first thing we like to talk about is inflation, and how we can account for rising prices to help our clients keep their standard of living level in retirement. We look for products that can be "turned on" later in their retirement plans to achieve their goals. We also look at anticipated cash infusions later in their lives, such as an inheritance or the sale of property.

I can't count the number of times I have sat with a couple, asked them about their spending, and heard them throw out a number that seemed incredibly low. When I ask them where the number came from, they usually say they estimated based on their total bills. Yet, our spending is so much more than our mortgage, utilities, cable, phone, car, grocery, or credit card bills.

"What about clothes?" I ask, "Or dining out? What about gifts and coffees and last-minute birthday cards?" That's when the lights come on.

This is why I suggest collecting a year's worth of information. There is usually no such thing as a one-time purchase. Did you buy new furniture? Even if that is a rarity, do you think that will be the last time you *ever* buy furniture?

We've had several clients over the years who've told us they expected to need very little to live on in retirement, only to learn they could live on four times as much as they'd planned to spend and still never outlive their money. On the other hand, we've also had clients who underestimated their expenses in retirement, and found out that they do not have enough to live on during their golden years. Our firm believes that it is important to accurately estimate what the client's retirement expenses will be, and make that part of their *Roadmap*, so that there are no surprises down the road.

Another hefty expense is spending on the kids. Many of the couples I work with are quick to help their adult children, whether it's something like letting them live in the basement, paying for college, babysitting, paying an occasional bill, or contributing to a grandchild's college fund. They aren't alone—more than half of parents with a child over eighteen provide them financial support. And it's not unlikely for some parents to tap into their retirement funds to do so.[18]

---

[18] Jessica Dickler. CNBC. April 25, 2022. "Half of parents still financially support their adult children, study shows." https://www.cnbc.com/2022/04/25/half-of-parents-still-financially-support-adult-children-study-shows.html

My clients sometimes protest that what they do for their grown children can stop in retirement. They don't *need* to help. But I get it. Parents like to feel needed. And, while you never want to neglect saving for retirement in favor of taking on financial risks (like your child's student debt), the parents who help their adult children do so in part because it helps them feel fulfilled.

When it comes down to expenses, including (and especially) spending on your family, don't make your initial calculations based on what you *could* whittle your budget down to if you *had* to. Instead, start from where you are. Who wants to live off a bare-bones bank account in retirement?

Other Expenses

Once you have nailed down your current budget and your dreams or goals for retirement, there are a few other outstanding pieces to think about—some expenses many people don't take the time to consider before making and executing a plan. But I'm assuming you want to get it right, so let's take a look.

Housing

Do you know where you want to live in retirement? This makes up a substantial piece of your income puzzle—since the typical American household owns a home, and it's generally their largest asset.

Some people prefer to live right where they are for as long as they can. Others have been waiting for retirement to pull the trigger on an ambitious move, like purchasing a new house, or even downsizing. Whatever your plans and whatever your reasons, there are quite a few things to consider.

Mortgage

Do you still have a mortgage? What may have been a nice tax boon in your working years could turn into a financial burden in your retirement. After all, when you are on a limited income, a mortgage is just one more bill sapping your financial strength. It is something to put some thought into, whether you plan to age in place or are considering moving to your dream home, buying a house out of state, or living in a retirement community.

Upkeep and Taxes

A house without a mortgage still requires annual taxes. While it's tempting to think of this as a once-a-year expense, when you have limited earning potential, your annual tax bill might be something into which you should put a little more forethought.

The costs of homeownership aren't just monetary. When you find yourself dealing with more house than you need, it can drain your time and energy. From keeping clutter at bay to keeping the lawn mower running, upkeep can be extensive and expensive. For some, that's a challenge they heartily accept and can comfortably take on. For others, the idea of yard work or cleaning an area larger than they need feels foolish.

For instance, Peggy discovered after her knee replacement that most of her house was inaccessible to her when she was laid up.

"It felt ridiculous to pay someone else to dust and vacuum a house I was only living in 40 percent of!"

Practicality and Adaptability

Erik and Magda are looking to retire within the next two decades. They just sold their old three-bedroom ranch-style house. Their twins are in high school, and the couple has wanted to "upgrade" for years. Now they live in a gorgeous 1940s three-story house with all the kitchen space they ever wanted, five sprawling bedrooms, and a library and media room for themselves and their children. Within months of moving in, the couple realized a house perfect for their active teens would no longer be perfect for them in five to fifteen years.

"We are paying the mortgage for this house, but we've started saving for the next one," said Magda, "because who wants to climb two flights of stairs to their bedroom when they're seventy-eight?"

Others I know have encountered similar situations in their personal lives. After a health crisis, one couple found the luxurious tub for two they toiled to install had become a specter of a bad slip and a potential safety risk. It's important to think through what your physical reality could be, whatever your long-term plan might be; it's amazing how many people don't.

Contracts and Regulations

If you are looking into a cross-country move, be aware of new tax tables or local ordinances in the area where you are looking to move. After all, you don't want to experience sticker-shock when you are looking at downsizing or reducing your bills in retirement.

Along the same lines, if you are moving into a retirement community, be sure to look at the fine print. What happens if you must move into a different situation for long-term care? Will you be penalized? Will you be responsible for replacing your slot in the community? What are all the fees, and what do they cover?

When you buy into a retirement community that will take care of you for the rest of your life, you're paying for the condo or cottage you're living in, and you pay homeowner's association fees to provide for the upkeep of the property. We've seen monthly fees of $800-$900 or more, which can really drain your retirement. That's a lot of money to pay to have your grass mowed and your light bulbs changed! There are valuable services provided, but you can do a lot of things for $12,000 a year which might be more cost-effective.

Inflation

As I write this in 2021, America had experienced a long stretch of low inflation. Inflation had not exceeded 4 percent since 1991 until that 30-year run ended with readings exceeding 4 percent in April 2021.[19]

However, inflation isn't a one-time bump; it has a cumulative effect. Even with relatively low inflation over the past few decades, the $20 sneakers you bought your grade-schooler in 1991 will cost $37.90 to buy for your grandchild today.[20] What if, in retirement, we hit a stretch like the late '70s and early '80s, when annual inflation rates of 10 percent became the norm? It may be wise to consider some extra padding in your retirement income plan to account for any potential increase in inflation in the future.

Aging

Also, in the expense category, think about longevity. We all hope to age gracefully. However, it's important to face the prospect of aging with a sense of realism.

The elephant in the room for many families is long-term care: No one wants to admit they will likely need it, but estimates say as many as 70 percent of us will.[21] Aging is a significant piece of retirement income planning because you'll want to figure out how to set aside money for your care, either at home or away from it. The more comfortable you get with

---

[19] US Inflation Calculator. January 2021. "Historical Inflation Rates." http://www.usinflationcalculator.com/inflation/historical-inflation-rates/
[20] Ibid.
[21] Moll Law Group. 2021. "The Cost of Long-Term Care." https://www.molllawgroup.com/the-cost-of-long-term-care.html

discussing your wishes and plans with your loved ones, the easier planning for the financial side of it can be.

I discuss health care and potential long-term care costs in more detail elsewhere in this book, but, suffice it to say, nursing home care tends to be very expensive and typically isn't something you get to choose when you will need.

It isn't just the costs of long-term care that pose a concern in living longer. It's also about covering the possible costs of everything else associated with living longer. For instance, if Henry retires from his job as a biochemical engineer at age sixty-five, perhaps he planned to have a very decent income for twenty years, until age eighty-five. But what if he lives until he's ninety-five? That's a whole third—ten years—more of personal income he will need.

Putting It All Together

Whew! So, you have pulled together what you have, and you have a pretty good idea of where you want to be. Now your financial professional and you can go about the work of arranging what assets you *have* to cover what you *need*—and how you might try to cover any gaps.

Like the proverbial man in the Bible who built his house on a rock, I like to help my clients figure out how to cover their day-to-day living expenses—their needs—with insurance and other guaranteed income sources like pensions and Social Security.

We use a *Roadmap* approach. We look at the three pillars of a financial plan, including Social Security, pension, and retirement and personal savings. Then we put together a plan that is going to calculate inflation at a given rate and show them how long the money could last. For most people, they are surprised to find that they have nothing to worry about. We find most people are relieved when we share the plan with them. They tell me they can now sleep better at night knowing they have a *Roadmap to Retirement*.

Again, you should keep in mind there isn't one single financial vehicle, asset, or source to fill all your needs, and that's okay. One of the challenges of planning for your income in retirement concerns figuring out what products and strategies to use. You can release some of that stress when you accept the fact you will need a diverse portfolio, not just one massive money pile.

One way to help shore up your income gaps is by working with your financial professional and a qualified tax advisor to mitigate your tax exposure. Effective tax planning isn't necessarily about "adding" to your income. Especially regarding retirement, it's less about what you make than it is about what you keep. Paying a lower tax bill keeps more money in your pocket, which is where you want it when it comes to retirement income.

Now you can look at ways to cover your remaining retirement goals. Are there products like long-term care insurance specific to a certain kind of expense you anticipate? Is there a particular asset you want to use for your "play" money—money for trips and gifts for the grandkids? Is there any way you can portion off money for those charitable legacy plans?

Once you have analyzed your income wants, needs, and the assets to realistically cover them, you may have a gap. The masterstroke of a competent financial professional will be to help you figure out how you will cover that gap. Will you need to cut out a round of golf a week? Maybe skip the new car? Or will you need to take more substantial action?

One way to cover an income gap is to consider working longer or even part-time before retirement and even after that magical calendar date. This may not be the best "plan" for you; disabilities, work demands, and physical or emotional limitations can hinder the best-laid plans to continue working. However, if it is physically possible for you, this is one considerable way to help your assets last, for more than one reason.

In fact, 26.6 percent of Americans between the ages of sixty-five and seventy-four are still working and 7.4 percent over the age of seventy-five.[22] While some do list their personal finances as a reason for staying on the job, others do so to avoid feeling bored in retirement, among other reasons.

I had a client, "Jane," who lost her husband and had a lot of medical expenses. She told me she thought she needed to work until age seventy-five, and she was only sixty-four. We reviewed her situation; with some planning, and some guaranteed returns, we discovered that Jane could retire at age sixty-six and never need to worry about working again.

When you're retired, you no longer have an employer paying you a steady check. It is up to you to make sure you have saved and planned for the income you need.

---

[22] U.S. Bureau of Labor Statistics. September 8, 2021. "Civilian labor force participation rate by age, sex, race, and ethnicity." https://www.bls.gov/emp/tables/civilian-labor-force-participation-rate.htm

CHAPTER 5

Social Security

Social Security is often the foundation of retirement income. Backed by the strength of the U.S. Treasury, it provides perhaps the most dependable paycheck you will have in retirement.

From the time you collect your first paycheck from the job that made you a bonafide taxpayer (for me, it was as a pizzamaker at Pizza Hut making $3.35 an hour—that was the minimum wage, with taxes still being taken out of that) you are paying into the grand old Social Security system. What grew and developed out of the pressures of the Great Depression has become one of the most popular government programs in the country, and, if you pay in for the equivalent of ten years or more, you, too, can benefit from the Social Security program.

Now, before we get into the nitty-gritty of Social Security, I'd like to address a current concern: Will Social Security still be there for you when you reach retirement age?

The Future of Social Security

This question is ever-present as headlines trumpet an underfunded Social Security program, alongside the sea of baby boomers who are retiring in droves and the comparatively smaller pool of younger people who are bearing the responsibility of funding the system.

The Social Security Administration itself acknowledges this concern as each Social Security statement now bears an asterisk that continues near the end of the summary:

> "*Your estimated benefits are based on current law. Congress has made changes to the law in the past and can do so at any time. The law governing benefit amounts may change because, by 2034, the payroll taxes collected will be enough to pay only about 79 percent of scheduled benefits."

Just a reminder, as if you needed one, that nothing in life is guaranteed. Additionally, depending on who you're listening to, Social Security funds may run low before 2034 thanks to the financial instability and government spending that accompanied the 2020 COVID-19 pandemic.

Before you get too discouraged, though, here are a few thoughts to keep you going:

- Even if the program is only paying 79 cents on the dollar for scheduled benefits, 79 percent is notably not zero.
- The Social Security Administration has made changes in the distant and near past to protect the fund's solvency, including increasing retirement ages and striking certain filing strategies.
- There are many changes Congress could make, and lawmakers are currently discussing how to fix the system, such as further increasing full retirement age and eligibility.
- One thing no one is seriously discussing? Reneging on current obligations to retirees or the soon-to-retire.

Take heart. The real answer to the question, "Will Social Security be there for me?" is still yes.

This question is an important one to consider when you look at how much we, as a nation, rely on this program. Did you know Social Security benefits replace about 40 percent of a person's original income when they retire?[23]

If you ask me, that's a pretty significant piece of your retirement income puzzle.

Another caveat? You may not realize this, but no one can legally "advise" you about your Social Security benefits.

"But, Bill," you may be thinking, "isn't that part of what you do? And what about that nice gentleman at the Social Security Administration office I spoke with on the phone?"

Don't get me wrong. Social Security Administration employees know their stuff. They are trained to know policies and programs, and they are usually pretty quick to tell you what you can and cannot do. But the government specifically says, because Social Security is a benefit you alone have paid into and earned, your Social Security decisions, too, are yours alone.

When it comes to financial professionals, we can't push you in any directions, either, *but*—there's a big but here—working with a well-informed financial professional is still incredibly handy when it comes to your Social Security decisions. Why? Because someone who's worth his or her salt will know what withdrawal strategies might pertain to your specific situation and will ask questions that can help you determine what you are looking for when it comes to your Social Security.

For instance, some people want the highest possible monthly benefit. Others want to start their benefits early, not always because of financial need. I heard about one man who called in to start his Social Security payments the day he qualified, just because he liked to think of it as the government paying back a debt it owed him, and he enjoyed the feeling of receiving a check from Uncle Sam.

Whatever your reasons, questions, or feelings regarding Social Security, the decision is yours alone; but working with a financial professional can help you put your options in

---

[23] Social Security Administration. "Learn About Social Security Programs." https://www.ssa.gov/planners/retire/r&m6.html

perspective by showing you—both with industry knowledge and with proprietary software or planning processes—where your benefits fit into your overall strategy for retirement income.

One reason the federal government doesn't allow for "advice" related to Social Security, I suspect, is so no one can profit from giving you advice related to your Social Security benefit—or from providing any clarifications. Again, this is a sign of a good financial professional. Those who are passionate about their work will be knowledgeable about what benefit strategies might be to your advantage and will happily share those possible options with you.

Full Retirement Age

When it comes to Social Security, it seems like many people only think so far as "yes." They don't take the time to understand the various options available. Instead, because it is common knowledge you can begin your benefits at age sixty-two, that's what many of us do. While more people are opting to delay taking benefits, age sixty-two is still firmly the most popular age to start.[24]

What many people fail to understand is, by starting benefits early, they may be leaving a lot of money on the table. You see, the Social Security Administration bases your monthly benefit on two factors: your earnings history and your full retirement age (FRA).

From your earnings history, they pull the thirty-five years you made the most money and use a mathematical indexing formula to figure out a monthly average from those years. If you paid into the system for less than thirty-five years, then every year you didn't pay in will be counted as a zero.

---

[24] Chris Kissell. moneytalknews.com. January 20, 2021. "This Is When the Most People Start Taking Social Security."
https://www.moneytalksnews.com/the-most-popular-age-for-claiming-social-security/

Once they have calculated what your monthly earning would be at FRA, the government then calculates what to put on your check based on how close you are to FRA. FRA was originally set at sixty-five, but, as the population aged and lifespans lengthened, the government shifted FRA later and later, based on an individual's year of birth. Check out the following chart to see when you will reach FRA.[25]

---

[25] Social Security Administration. "Full Retirement Age." https://www.ssa.gov/planners/retire/retirechart.html

Age to Receive Full Social Security Benefits*

(Called "full retirement age" [FRA] or "normal retirement age.")

Year of Birth*	FRA
1937 or earlier	65
1938	65 and 2 months
1939	65 and 4 months
1940	65 and 6 months
1941	65 and 8 months
1942	65 and 10 months
1943-1954	66
1955	66 and 2 months
1956	66 and 4 months
1957	66 and 6 months
1958	66 and 8 months
1959	66 and 10 months
1960 and later	67

If you were born on Jan. 1 of any year, you should refer to the previous year. (If you were born on the 1st of the month, we figure your benefit [and your full retirement age] as if your birthday was in the previous month.)

When you reach FRA, you are eligible to receive 100 percent of whatever the Social Security Administration says is your full monthly benefit.

Starting at age sixty-two, for every year before FRA you claim benefits, your monthly check is reduced by 5 percent or more. Conversely, for every year you delay taking benefits past FRA, your monthly benefit increases by 8 percent (until age seventy—after that, there is no monetary advantage to delaying Social Security benefits). While your circumstances and needs may vary, a lot of financial professionals still urge people to at least consider delaying until they reach age seventy.

Why Wait?[26]

\multicolumn{9}{c	}{Taking benefits early could affect your monthly check by _____.}
62	63	64	65	FRA 66	67	68	69	70
-25%	-20%	-13.3%	-6.7%	0	+8%	+16%	+24%	+32%

My Social Security

If you are over age thirty, you have probably received a notice from the Social Security Administration telling you to activate something called "My Social Security." This is a handy way to learn more about your particular benefit options, to keep track of what your earnings record looks like, and to calculate the benefits you have accrued over the years.

Essentially, My Social Security is an online account you can activate to see what your personal Social Security picture looks like, which you can do at www.ssa.gov/myaccount. This can be extremely helpful when it comes to planning for income in

---

[26] Social Security Administration. April 2021. "Can You Take Your Benefits Before Full Retirement Age?"
https://www.ssa.gov/planners/retire/applying2.html

retirement and figuring up the difference between your anticipated income versus anticipated expenses.

My Social Security is also helpful because it's a great way to see if there is a problem. For instance, I have heard of one woman who, through diligently checking her tax records against her Social Security profile, discovered her Social Security check was shortchanging her, based on her earnings history. After taking the discrepancy to the Social Security Administration, they sent her what they owed her in makeup benefits.

COLA

Social Security is a largely guaranteed piece of the retirement puzzle: If you get a statement that says to expect $1,000 a month, you can be sure you will receive $1,000 a month. But there is one variable detail, and that is something called the cost-of-living adjustment, or COLA.

The COLA is an increase in your monthly check meant to address inflation in everyday life. After all, your expenses will likely continue to experience inflation in retirement, but you will no longer have the opportunity for raises, bonuses, or promotions you had when you were working. Instead, Social Security receives an annual cost-of-living increase tied to the Department of Labor's Consumer Price Index for Urban Wage Earners and Clerical Workers, or CPI-W. If the CPI-W measurement shows inflation rose a certain amount for regular goods and services, then Social Security recipients will see that reflected in their COLA.

The COLA averages 4 percent, but in a no- or low-inflation environment, such as in 2010, 2011, and 2016, Social Security recipients will not receive an adjustment. Some view the COLA as a perk, bump, or bonus, but, in reality, it works more like this: Your mom sends you to the store with $2.50 for a gallon of milk. Milk costs exactly $2.50. The next week, you go back with that same amount, but it is now $2.52 for a gallon, so you go back to Mom, and she gives you 2 cents. You aren't bringing home more milk—it just costs more money.

So the COLA is less about "making more money" and more about keeping seniors' purchasing power from eroding when inflation is a big factor, such as in 1975, when it was 8 percent![27] Still, don't let that detract from your enthusiasm about COLAs; after all, what if Mom's solution was: "Here's the same $2.50; try to find pennies from somewhere else to get that milk!"?

Spousal Benefits

We've talked about FRA, but another big Social Security decision involves spousal benefits.

If you or your spouse has a long stretch of zeros in your earnings history—perhaps if one of you stayed home for years, caring for children or sick relatives—you may want to consider filing for spousal benefits instead of filing on your own earnings history. A spousal benefit can be up to 50 percent of the primary wage earner's benefit at full retirement age.

To begin drawing a spousal benefit, you must be at least sixty-two years old, and the primary wage earner must have already filed for his or her benefit. While there are penalties for taking spousal benefits early (you could lose up to 67.5 percent of your check for filing at age sixty-two), you cannot earn credits for delaying past full retirement age. [28]

Like I said, the spousal benefit can be a big deal for those who don't have a very long pay history, but it's important to weigh your own earned benefits against the option of withdrawing based on a fraction of your spouse's benefits.

---

[27] Social Security Administration. "Cost-Of-Living Adjustment (COLA) Information for 2021." https://www.ssa.gov/cola/.
[28] Social Security Administration. "Retirement Planner: Benefits For You As A Spouse." https://www.ssa.gov/planners/retire/applying6.html

To look at how this could play out, let's use a hypothetical example of Mary Jane, who is sixty, and Peter, who is sixty-two.

Let's say Peter's benefit at FRA, in his case sixty-six, would be $1,600. If Peter begins his benefits right now, four years before FRA, his monthly check will be $1,200. If Mary Jane begins taking spousal benefits in two years at the earliest date possible, her monthly benefits will be reduced by 67.5 percent, to $520 per month (remember, at FRA, the most she can qualify for is half of Peter's FRA benefit).

What if Peter and Mary Jane both wait until FRA? At sixty-six, Peter begins taking his full benefit of $1,600 a month. Two years later, when she reaches age sixty-six, Mary Jane will qualify for $800 a month. By waiting until FRA, the couple's monthly benefit goes from $1,720 to $2,400.

What if Peter delays until age seventy to get his maximum possible benefit? For each year past FRA he delays, his monthly benefits increase by 8 percent. This means, at seventy, he could file for a monthly benefit of $2,112. However, delayed retirement credits do not affect spousal benefits, so as soon as Peter files at seventy, Mary Jane would also file (at age sixty-eight) for her maximum benefit of $800, so their highest possible combined monthly check is $2,912.[29]

When it comes to your Social Security benefits, you obviously will want to consider whether a monthly check based on a fraction of your spouse's earnings will be comparable to or larger than your own earnings history.

Divorced Spouses

There are a few considerations for those of us who have gone through a divorce. If you 1) were married for ten years or more *and* 2) have since been divorced for at least two years *and* 3)

---

[29] Office of the Chief Actuary. Social Security Administration. "Social Security Benefits: Benefits for Spouses."
https://www.ssa.gov/OACT/quickcalc/spouse.html#calculator

are unmarried *and* 4) your ex-spouse qualifies to begin Social Security, you qualify for a spousal benefit based on your ex-husband or ex-wife's earnings history at FRA. A divorced spousal benefit is different from the married spousal benefit in one way: You don't have to wait for your ex-spouse to file before you can file yourself.[30]

For instance, Charles and Moira were married for fifteen years before their divorce, when he was thirty-six and she was forty. Moira has been remarried for twenty years, and, although Charles briefly remarried, his second marriage ended after a few years. Charles' benefits are largely calculated based on his many years of volunteering in schools, meaning his personal monthly benefit is close to zero.

Although Moira has deferred her retirement, opting to delay benefits until she is seventy, Charles can begin taking benefits calculated from Moira's work history at FRA as early as sixty-two. However, he will also have the option of waiting until FRA to collect the maximum, or 50 percent of Moira's earned monthly benefit at her FRA.

Widowed Spouses

If your marriage ended with the death of your spouse, you might claim a benefit for your spouse's earned income as his or her widow/widower, called a survivor's benefit. Unlike a spousal benefit or divorced benefits, if your husband or wife dies, you can claim his or her full benefit. Also, unlike spousal benefits, if you need to, you can begin taking income when you turn sixty. However, as with other benefit options, your monthly check will be permanently reduced for withdrawing benefits before FRA.

If your spouse began taking benefits before he or she died, you can't delay withdrawing your survivor's benefits to get

---

[30] Social Security Administration. "Retirement Planner: If You Are Divorced." https://www.ssa.gov/planners/retire/divspouse.html

delayed credits; the Social Security Administration says you can only get as much from a survivor's benefit as your deceased spouse might have gotten, had he or she lived.[31]

Taxes, Taxes, Taxes

With Social Security, as with everything, it is important to consider taxes. It may be surprising, but your Social Security benefits are not tax-free. Despite having been taxed to accrue those benefits in the first place, you may have to pay Uncle Sam income taxes on up to 85 percent of your Social Security.

The Social Security Administration figures these taxes using what they call "the provisional income formula." Your provisional income formula differs from the adjusted gross income you use for your regular income taxes. Instead, to find out how much of your Social Security benefit is taxable, the Social Security Administration calculates it this way:

Provisional Income = Adjusted Gross Income + Nontaxable Interest + ½ of Social Security

See that piece about nontaxable interest? That generally means interest from government bonds and notes. It surprises many people that, although you may not pay taxes on those assets, their income will count against you when it comes to Social Security taxation.

Once you have figured out your provisional income (also called "combined income"), you can use the following chart to figure out your Social Security taxes.[32]

---

[31] Social Security Administration. "Social Security Benefit Amounts For The Surviving Spouse By Year Of Birth." https://www.ssa.gov/planners/survivors/survivorchartred.html

[32] Social Security Administration. "Benefits Planner: Income Taxes and Your Social Security Benefits." https://www.ssa.gov/planners/taxes.html

Taxes on Social Security

Provisional Income = Adjusted Gross Income + Nontaxable Interest + ½ of Social Security

If you are ___ and your provisional income is___, then...		Uncle Sam will tax ___ of your Social Security
Single	Married, filing jointly	
Less than $25,000	Less than $32,000	0%
$25,000 to $34,000	$32,000 to $44,000	Up to 50%
More than $34,000	More than $44,000	Up to 85%

This is one more reason it may benefit you to work with financial and tax professionals: They can look at your entire financial picture to make your overall retirement approach as tax-efficient as possible—including your Social Security benefit.

Working and Social Security: The Earnings Test

If you haven't reached FRA, but you started your Social Security benefits and are still working, things get a little hairy.

Because you have started Social Security payments, the Social Security Administration will pay out your benefits (at that reduced rate, of course, because you haven't reached your FRA). Yet, because you are working, the organization must also withhold from your check to add to your benefits, which you are already collecting. See how this complicates matters?

To straighten the situation, the government has what is called the earnings test. For 2021, you can earn up to $18,960 without it affecting your Social Security check. But, for every $2 you earn past that amount, the Social Security Administration will withhold $1. The earnings test loosens in the year of your FRA; if you are reaching FRA in 2021, you can earn up to $51,540 before you run into the earnings test, and the government only withholds $1 for every $3 past that amount. The month you reach FRA, you are no longer subject to any earnings withholding. For instance, if you are still working and turned sixty-six by December 28, 2021, you would only have to worry about the earnings test until December, and then you can ignore it entirely. Keep in mind, the money the government withholds from your Social Security benefits while you are working before FRA will be tacked back onto your benefits check after FRA.[33]

We help clients figure out how much Social Security they will get at any age after sixty-two. We can project their individual numbers and the income for their spouse. We show them the advantage of waiting until full Social Security age and explain how many years they would need to live to make up the income they could have gotten had they started it earlier. Clients are usually surprised to learn that starting their Social Security payments early means it will take them approximately fourteen years to catch up. If longevity runs in your family, then we say take it later. If not, we say take it earlier. None of us has a crystal ball to know when the exact time is, but when we are looking at a client's complete picture, we can help them figure out the ideal time to start their Social Security benefits.

---

[33] Social Security Administration. "Exempt Amounts Under the Earnings Test." https://www.ssa.gov/oact/cola/rtea.html

CHAPTER 6

401(k)s & IRAs

Have you heard? Today's retirement is not your parents' retirement. You see, back in the day, it was pretty common to work for one company for the vast majority of your career and then retire with a gold watch and a pension.

The gold watch was a symbol of the quality time you had put in at that company, but the pension was more than a symbol. Instead, it was a guarantee—as solid as your employer—that they would repay your hard work with a certain amount of income in your old age. Did you see the caveat there? Your pension's guarantee was *as solid as your employer*. The problem was, what if your employer went under?

Companies that failed couldn't pay their retired employees' pensions, leading to financial challenges for many. Beginning in 1974 with Congress' passage of the Employee Retirement Income Security Act, federal legislation and regulations aimed at protecting retirees were everywhere. One piece of legislation included a relatively obscure section of the Internal Revenue Code, added in 1978. Section 401(k), to be specific.

IRC section 401, subsection k, created tax advantages for employer-sponsored financial products, even if the main contributor was the employee him or herself. Over the years, more employers took note, beginning an age of transition away from pensions and toward 401(k) plans. A 401(k) is a retirement account with certain tax benefits and restrictions on the investments or other financial products inside of it.

Essentially, 401(k)s and their individual retirement account (IRA) counterparts are "wrappers" that provide tax benefits around assets; typically, the assets that compose IRAs and 401(k)s are mutual funds, stock and bond mixes, and money market accounts. However, IRA and 401(k) contents are becoming more diverse these days, with some companies offering different kinds of annuity options within their plans.

Where pensions are defined-*benefit* plans, 401(k)s and IRAs are defined-*contribution* plans. The one-word change outlines the basic difference. Pensions spell out what you can expect to receive from the plan but not necessarily how much money it will take to fund those benefits. With 401(k)s, an employer sets a standard for how much they will contribute (if any), and you can be certain of what you are contributing. Still, there is no outline for what you can expect to receive in return for those contributions.

Modern employment looks very different. A 2018 survey by the Bureau of Labor Statistics determined U.S. workers stayed with their employers a median of about four years. Workers ages fifty-five to sixty-four had a little more staying power and were most likely to stay with their employer for about ten years.[34] Additionally, the outlook on the benefits front is different today, too. In 1979, 38 percent of workers had pensions. But 401(k)s are rising in number, with about 60 million American workers enrolled in a plan.[35]

A far cry from a pension and gold watch, wouldn't you say?

Preparing for retirement with a pension is completely different from planning a retirement without a pension. When you have a pension, you know the numbers you will get, for both you and your spouse, for the rest of your lives. You have

---

[34] Bureau of Labor Statistics. September 22, 2020. "Employee Tenure in 2020." https://www.bls.gov/news.release/pdf/tenure.pdf

[35] Investment Company Institute. June 30, 2021. "Frequently Asked Questions about 401(k) Plan Research." https://www.ici.org/policy/retirement/plan/401k/faqs_401k

an extra leg to stand on with your 401(k) plans and your Social Security checks. Pensions don't take into consideration the cost of living or future inflation. However, a pension provides a solid foundation, with a known future income amount, which gives clients more security in retirement.

If there is anything to learn from this paradigm shift, it's that you must look out for yourself. Whether you have worked for a company for two years or twenty, you are still the one who has to look out for your own best interests. That holds doubly true when it comes to preparing for retirement. If you are one of the lucky ones who still has a pension, good for you. But for the rest of us, it is likely a 401(k)—or possibly one of its nonprofit- or government-sector counterparts, a 403(b) or 457 plan—is one of your biggest assets for retirement.

Some employers offer incentives to contribute to their company plans, like a company match. On that subject, I have one thing to say: *Do it!* Nothing in life is free, as they say, but a company match on your retirement funds is about as close to free money as it gets. If you can make the minimum to qualify for your company's match at all, go for it.

Now, it's likely, during our working years, we mostly "set and forget" our 401(k) funding. Because it is tax-advantaged, your employer is taking money from your paycheck—before taxes—and putting it into your plan for you. Maybe you got to pick a selection of investments, or maybe your company only offers one choice of investment in your 401(k). But, when you are ready to retire or move jobs, you have choices to make requiring a little more thought and care.

When you are ready to part ways with your job, you have a few options:
- Leave the money where it is
- Take the cash (and pay income taxes and perhaps a 10 percent additional federal tax if you are younger than age fifty-nine-and-one-half)
- Transfer the money to another employer plan (if the new plan allows)

- Roll the money over into a self-directed IRA

Now, these are just general options. You will have to decide, with the help of a financial professional registered to provide investment advice, what's right for you.

Remember what we said earlier about how we change jobs more often these days? That means you likely have a 401(k) with your current company, but you may also have a string of retirement accounts trailing you from other jobs.

When it comes to your retirement income, it's important to be able to pull together *all* your assets, so you can examine what you have and where, and then decide what you will do with it.

Tax-Qualified, Tax-Preferred, Tax-Deferred ... Still TAXED

Financial media often cite IRAs and 401(k)s for their tax benefits. After all, with traditional plans, you put your money in, pre-tax, and it hopefully grows for years, even decades, untaxed. That's why these accounts are called "tax-qualified" or "tax-deferred" assets. They aren't *tax-free!* Rarely does Uncle Sam allow business to continue without receiving his piece of the pie, and your retirement assets are no different. If you didn't pay taxes on the front end, you will pay taxes on the money you withdraw from these accounts in retirement. Don't get me wrong: This isn't an inherently good or bad thing; it's just the way it is. It's important to understand, though, for the sake of planning ahead.

In retirement, many people assume they will be in a lower tax bracket. Are you planning to pare down your lifestyle in retirement? Perhaps you are, and perhaps you will have substantially less income in retirement. But many of my clients tell me they want to live life more or less the same as they always have. The money they would previously have spent on business attire or gas for their commute they now

ROADMAP TO RETIREMENT | 67

want to spend on hobbies and grandchildren. That's all fine, and for many of them, it is doable, but does it put them in a lower tax bracket? Probably not.

Keep in mind, IRAs, 401(k)s, and their alternatives have a few limitations because of their special tax status. For one thing, the IRS sets limits on your contributions to these retirement accounts. If you are contributing to a 401(k) or an equivalent nonprofit or government plan, your annual contribution limit is $19,500 (as of 2021). If you are fifty or older, the IRS allows additional contributions, called "catch-up contributions," of up to $6,500 on top of the regular limit of $19,500.[36] For an IRA, the limit is $6,000, with a catch-up limit of an additional $1,000. [37]

Because their tax advantages come from their intended use as retirement income, withdrawing funds from these accounts before you turn fifty-nine-and-one-half can carry stiff penalties. In addition to fees your investment management company might charge, you will have to pay income tax *and* a 10 percent federal tax penalty, with few exceptions.

The fifty-nine-and-one-half rule for retirement accounts is incredibly important to remember, especially when you're young.

Many millennials I see in my practice say, while they may be socking money away in their workplace retirement plan, it is often the *only* place they are saving. This could be problematic later because of the fifty-nine-and-one-half rule; what if you have an emergency? It is important to fund your retirement, but you need to access to emergency funds. This can help you avoid breaking into your retirement accounts

---

[36] Jackie Stewart. Kiplinger.com. February 5, 2021. "401(k) Contribution Limits for 2021" https://www.kiplinger.com/retirement/retirement-planning/602191/401k-contribution-limits-for-2021#:~:text=The%20maximum%20amount%20workers%20can,contributions%20for%202021%20to%20%2426%2C000.
[37] Fidelity.com. 2021. "IRA contribution limits" https://www.fidelity.com/retirement-ira/contribution-limits-deadlines

and incurring taxes and penalties as a result of the fifty-nine-and-one-half rule.

RMDs

Remember how we talked about the 401(k) or IRA being a "tax wrapper" for your funds? Well, eventually, Uncle Sam will want a bite of that candy bar. So, when you turn seventy-two, the government requires you withdraw a portion of your account, which the IRS calculates based on the size of your account and your estimated lifespan. This required minimum distribution, or RMD, is the government's insurance it will collect some taxes, at some point, from your earnings. Because you didn't pay taxes on the front end, you will now pay income taxes on whatever you withdraw, including your RMDs. Also, let me just remind you not to play chicken with the U.S. government; if you don't take your RMDs starting at seventy-two, you will have to write a check to the IRS for *50 percent* of the amount of your missed RMDs.

With the change in law from the SECURE Act of 2019, even after you begin RMDs, you can still also continue contributing to your 401(k) or IRAs if you are still employed, which can affect the whole discussion on RMDs and possible tax considerations.

If you don't need income from your retirement accounts, RMDs can seem like more of a tax burden than an income boon. While some people prefer to reinvest their RMDs, this comes with the possibility of additional taxation: You'll pay income taxes on your RMDs and then capital gains taxes on the growth of your investments. If you are legacy minded, there are other ways to use RMDs, many of which have tax benefits.

Permanent Life Insurance
One way to turn those pesky RMDs into a legacy is through permanent life insurance. Assuming you need the death

benefit coverage and can qualify for it medically, if properly structured, these products can pass on a sizeable death benefit to your beneficiaries, tax-free, as part of your general legacy plan.

ILIT
Another way to use RMDs toward your legacy is to work with an estate planning attorney to create an irrevocable life insurance trust (ILIT). This is basically a permanent life insurance policy placed within a trust. Because the trust is irrevocable, you would relinquish control of it, but, unlike with just a permanent life insurance policy, your death benefit won't count toward your taxable estate.

Annuities
Because annuities can be tax-deferred, using all or a portion of your RMDs to fund an annuity contract can be one way to further delay taxation while guaranteeing your income payments (either to you or your loved ones) later. (Assuming you don't need the income from the RMDs during your retirement.)

Qualified Charitable Distributions
If you are charity-minded, you may use your RMDs toward a charitable organization instead of using them for income. You must do this directly from your retirement account (you can't take the RMD check and *then* pay the charity) for your withdrawals to be qualified charitable distributions (QCDs), but this is one way of realizing some of the benefits of a charitable legacy during your own lifetime. You will not need to pay taxes on your QCDs, and they won't count toward your annual charitable tax deduction limit, plus you'll be able to see how the organization you are supporting uses your donations. You should consult a financial professional on how to

correctly make a QCD, particularly since the SECURE Act of 2019 has implemented a few regulations on this point.[38]

The way we mitigate tax consequences of RMDs is to point out what a client will have to take out in the future once they reach age seventy-two. By planning early in retirement, we show clients how to pay the tax over five years and never have to take an RMD during their lifetime. We convert their retirement savings to Roth IRAs or to life insurance contracts that they can take money from, tax free, for the rest of their lives. When we share with them these ideas, and show the future tax liability on all of their retirement money, most clients see that it is a no-brainer to convert and pay the tax today with known tax brackets.

Roth IRA

Since the Taxpayer Relief Act of 1997, there has been a different kind of retirement account, or "tax wrapper," available to the public: the Roth. Roth IRAs and Roth 401(k)s each differ from their traditional counterparts in one big way: You pay your taxes on the front end. This means, once your post-tax money is in the Roth account, as long as you follow the rules and limitations of that account, your distributions are truly tax-free. You won't pay income tax when you take withdrawals, so, in turn, you don't have to worry about RMDs. However, Roth accounts have the same limitations as traditional 401(k)s and IRAs when it comes to withdrawing money before age fifty-nine-and-one-half, with the added stipulation that the account must have been open for at least five years in order for the accountholder to make withdrawals.

---

[38] Bob Carlson. Forbes. January 28, 2020. "More Questions And Answers About The SECURE Act."
https://www.forbes.com/sites/bobcarlson/2020/01/28/more-questions-and-answers-about-the-secure-act/#113d49564869

Taking Charge

As mentioned earlier, the 401(k) and IRA have largely replaced pensions, but they aren't an equal trade.

Pensions are employer-funded; the money feeding into them is money that wouldn't ever show up on your pay stub. Because 401(k)s are self-funded, you must actively and consciously save. This distinction has made a difference when it comes to funding retirement. According to one NerdWallet article, the average 401(k) balance for a person age sixty to sixty-nine is $198,600, but the median likely tells the full story. The median 401(k) balance for a person age sixty to sixty-nine is $63,000. The article also cites the general suggestion to aim, by age thirty, to have saved up an amount equal to 50 percent to 100 percent of your annual salary.[39] For some thirty-year-olds, saving half an annual salary by age thirty is more than some sixty-to-sixty-nine-year-olds have saved for their entire lives

There can be many reasons why people underfund their retirement plans, like being overwhelmed by the investment choices or taking withdrawals from IRAs when they leave an employer, but the reason at the top of the list is this: People simply aren't participating to begin with.

So, no matter where you're saving with a private company, separate from your workplace, the most important retirement income decision you can make is to sock away your money somewhere in the first place.

---

[39] Arielle O'Shea. Nerd Wallet. March 17, 2021. "The Average 401(k) Balance by Age." https://www.nerdwallet.com/article/investing/the-average-401k-balance-by-age

CHAPTER 7

Annuities

In my practice, I offer my clients a variety of insurance products, all designed to help them reach their financial goals. You may be wondering: Why single out a single product in this book?

Well, while most of my clients have a pretty good understanding of business and finance, I sometimes find those who have the impression there must be magic involved. Some people assume there is a magic finance wand we can wave to change years' worth of savings into a strategy for retirement income. But it's not as easy as a goose laying golden eggs or the Fairy Godmother turning a pumpkin into a coach!

Finances aren't magic; it takes lots of hard work and, typically, several financial products and strategies to pull together a complete retirement plan. Of all the financial products I work with, it seems people find none more mysterious than annuities. And, if I may say, even some of those who recognize the word "annuity" have a limited understanding of the product. So, in the interest of demystifying annuities, let me tell you a little about what an annuity is.

In general, insurance is a financial hedge against risk. Car owners buy auto insurance to protect their finances in case they injure someone or someone injures them. Homeowners have house insurance to protect their finances in case of a fire, flood, or another disaster. People have life insurance to protect their finances in case of untimely death. Almost juxtaposed to life insurance, people have annuities in case of a long life; annuities can give you financial protection by providing consistent and reliable income payments.

The basic premise of an annuity is you, the annuitant, pay an insurance company some amount in exchange for their contractual guarantee they will pay you income for a certain time period. How that company pays you, for how long, and how much they offer are all determined by the annuity contract you enter into with the insurance company.

How You Get Paid

There are two ways for an annuity contract to provide income: The first is through what is called annuitization, and the second is through the use of income riders. We'll get into income riders in a bit, but let's talk about annuitization. That nice, long word is, in my opinion, one reason annuities have a reputation for mystery and misinformation.

Annuitization

When someone "annuitizes" a contract, it is the point where he or she turns on the income stream. Once a contract has been annuitized, there is no going back. With annuities, if the policyholder lives longer than the insurance company planned, the insurance company is still obligated to pay him or her, even if the payments end up being way more than the contract's actual value. If, however, the policyholder dies an untimely death, depending on the contract type, the insurance company may keep anything left of the money that funded the annuity—nothing would be paid out to the contract holder's survivors. You see where that could make some people balk?
Now, modern annuities rarely rely on annuitization for the income portion of the contract, and instead have so many bells and whistles that the old concept of annuitization seems

outdated, but because this is still an option, it's important to at least understand the basic concept.

Riders

Speaking of bells and whistles, let's talk about riders. Modern annuities have a lot of different options these days, many in the form of riders you can add to your contract for a fee—usually about 1 percent of the contract value per year. Each rider has its particulars, and the types of riders available will vary by the type of annuity contract purchased, but I'll just briefly outline some of these little extras:

- Lifetime income rider: Contract guarantees you an enhanced income for life
- Death benefit rider: Contract pays an enhanced death benefit to your beneficiaries even if you have annuitized
- Return of premium rider: Guarantees you (or your beneficiaries) will at least receive back the premium value of the annuity
- Long-term care rider: Provides a certain amount, sometimes as much as twice the principal value of the contract, to help pay for long-term care if the contract holder is moved to a nursing home or assisted living situation

This isn't an extensive look, and usually the riders have fancier names based on the issuing company, like "Lorem Ipsum Insurance Company Income Preferred Bonus Fixed Index Annuity rider," but I just wanted to show you what some of the general options are in layperson's terms.

Types of Annuities

Annuities break down into four basic types: immediate, variable, fixed, and fixed index.

Immediate

Immediate annuities primarily rely on annuitization to provide income—you give the insurance company a lump sum up front, and your payments begin immediately. Once you begin receiving income payments, the transaction is irreversible, and you no longer have access to your money in a lump sum. When you die, any remaining contract value is typically forfeited to the insurance company.

All other annuity contract types are "deferred" contracts, meaning you fund your policy as a lump sum or over a period of years and you give it the opportunity to grow over time—sometimes years, sometimes decades.

Variable

A variable annuity is an insurance contract as well as an investment. It's sold by insurance companies, but only through someone who is registered to sell investment products. With a variable annuity contract, the insurance company invests your premiums in subaccounts that are tied to the stock market. This makes it a bit different from the other annuity contract types because it is the only contract where your money is subject to losses because of market declines. Your contract value has a greater opportunity to grow, but it also stands to lose. Additionally, your contract's value will be subject to the underlying investment's fees and limitations—including capital gains taxes, management fees, etc. Once it is time for you to receive income from the contract, the insurance company will pay you a certain income, locked in at whatever your contract's value was.

We do not like variable annuities for several reasons. The first is illustrated by this example: If you had $100,000 and the market went down by 20 percent, you now have $80,000 as a living benefit and $100,000 as a death benefit. You cannot spend death benefit. Only your beneficiaries would do that. The other reason we don't like variable annuities is that they come with fees "inside" them. There are mortality and expense charges. There are sub-account fees. There are rider charges. These fees can range from 2 percent to as high as 6 percent. The variable annuity insurance companies are making money with these products no matter what happens to your money in the market. We've seen over the years that people can get "way upside down," meaning they put in $175,000 and later find their account value is only $100,000; then, because of market volatility, they have to hold these expensive contracts because of the death benefit. For these reasons, we aren't fond of variable annuity products for our clients.

Fixed

A traditional fixed annuity is pretty straightforward. You purchase a contract with a guaranteed interest rate and, when you are ready, the insurance company will make regular income payments to you at whatever payout rate your contract guarantees. Those payments will continue for the rest of your life and, if you choose, for the remainder of your spouse's life.

Fixed annuities don't have much in the way of upside potential, but many people like them for their guarantees (after all, if your Aunt May lives to be ninety-five, knowing she has a paycheck later in life can be her mental and financial safety net), as well as for their predictability. Unlike variable annuities, which are subject to market risk and might be up one year and down the next, you can easily calculate the value of your fixed annuity over your lifetime.

Fixed Index

To recap, variable annuities take on more risk to offer more possibilities to grow. Fixed annuities have less potential growth, but they protect your principal. In the last couple of decades, many insurance companies have retooled their product line to offer fixed index annuities, which are sort of midway between variable and fixed annuities on that risk/reward spectrum. Fixed index annuities offer greater growth potential than traditional fixed annuities but less than variable annuities. Like traditional fixed annuities, however, fixed index annuities are protected from downside market losses.

Fixed index annuities earn interest that is tied to the market, meaning that, instead of your contract value growing at a set interest rate like a traditional fixed annuity, it has the potential to grow within a range. Your contract's value is credited interest based on the performance of an external market index like the S&P 500 while never being invested in the market itself. You can't invest in the S&P 500 directly, but each year, your annuity as the potential to earn interest based on the chosen index's performance, submit to limits set by the company such as caps, spreads and participation rates. For instance, if your contract caps your interest at 5 percent, then in a year that the S&P 500 gains 3 percent, your annuity value increases 3 percent. If the S&P 500 gains 35 percent, your annuity value gets a 5 percent interest bump. But since your money isn't actually invested in the market with a fixed index annuity, if the market nosedives (such as happened during 2000, 2008 and 2020, anyone?) you won't see any increase in your contract value. Conversely, there will also be no decrease in your contract value—no matter how badly the market performed, as long as you follow the terms of the contract, you won't lose any of the interest you were credited in previous years. So, what if the S&P 500 shows a market loss of 30 percent? Your contract value isn't going anywhere (unless you purchased an optional rider—this charge will still come out of your annuity value each year). For those who are more interested in protection than growth potential, fixed index annuities can be an attractive option because, when the stock market has a long period of positive performance, a fixed index annuity can enjoy conservative growth. And, during stretches where the stock market is erratic and stock values across the board take significant losses? Fixed index annuities won't lose anything due to the stock market volatility.

There are several ways we use fixed index annuities in our practice. We use them for accumulation, or for income-generating guarantees. Clients like knowing they cannot lose any money due to market volatility. In the worst-case scenario, as mentioned earlier, they "get a zero" and keep all their gains and original principle, even during market downturns. They also like knowing that they can turn on income streams when they are ready and can never outlive those income streams, which gives our clients true peace of mind in retirement.

Other Things to Know About Annuities

We just talked about the four kinds of annuity contracts available, but all of them have some commonalities as annuities.

For all annuities, the contractual guarantees are only as strong as the insurance company that sells the product, which makes it important to thoroughly check the credit ratings of any company whose products you are considering.

Annuities are tax-deferred, meaning you don't have to pay taxes on interest earnings each year as the contract value grows. Instead, you will pay ordinary income taxes on your withdrawals. These are meant to be long-term products, so, like other tax-deferred or tax-advantaged products, if you begin taking withdrawals from your contract before age fifty-nine-and-one-half, you may also have to pay a 10 percent federal tax penalty. Also, while annuities are generally considered illiquid, most contracts allow you to withdraw up to 10 percent of your contract value every year. Withdraw any more, however, and you could incur additional surrender penalties.

Keep in mind, your withdrawals will deplete the accumulated cash value, death benefit, and, possibly, the rider values of your contract.

We use annuities in our practice because of what they offer: Security on the downside, with peace of mind that clients can't lose any of the gains they made when the market was cooperating.

One of our clients wanted an income stream. We were able to show them how they could get an income and pay less in taxes. We gave them an income stream of $24,000 a year and only 8 percent was included on their tax return. We took the remainder of their nest egg ($370,000) and put it into three tax-deferred annuities that could come due at different times. They could now take income in the future for the rest of their life.

Annuities aren't for everyone, but it's important to understand them before saying "yea" or "nay" on whether they fit into your plan; otherwise, you're not operating with complete information, wouldn't you agree? Regardless, you should talk to a financial professional who can help you understand annuities, help you dissect your particular financial needs, and help show you whether an annuity is appropriate for your retirement income plan.

CHAPTER 8

Estate & Legacy

In my practice, I devote a significant portion of my time to estate matters. That doesn't mean drawing up wills or trusts or putting together powers of attorney or anything like that. After all, I'm not an estate planning attorney. But I am a financial professional, and what part of the "estate" isn't affected by money matters?

I've included this chapter because I have seen many people do estate planning wrong. Clients, or clients' families, have come in after experiencing a death in the family and have found themselves in the middle of probate, high taxes, or a discovery of something unforeseen (often long-term care) draining the estate.

I have also seen people do estate planning right: clients or families who visit my office to talk about legacies and how to make them last and adult children who have room to grieve without an added burden of unintended costs, without stress from a family ruptured because of inadequate planning.

I'll share some of these stories here. However, I'm not going to give you specific advice, since everyone's situation is unique. I only want to give you some things to think about and to underscore the importance of planning ahead.

We work with elder law attorneys to help our clients keep more of their hard-earned money and leave less for the IRS or nursing homes. As mentioned earlier, we believe there is a strategy for the informed and a strategy for the uninformed.

By utilizing an elder law attorney, our clients are among the informed. They are advised of all the legal strategies that help clients keep more for their loved ones.

You Can't Take It With You

When it comes to legacy and estate planning, the most important thing is to *do it*. I have heard people from clients to celebrities (rap artist Snoop Dogg comes to mind) say they aren't interested in what happens to their assets when they die because they'll be dead. That's certainly one way to look at it. But I think that's a very selfish way to go about things—we all have people and causes we care about, and those who care about us. Even if the people we love don't *need* what we leave behind, they can still be fined or legally tied up in the probate process or burial costs if we don't plan for those. And that's not even considering what happens if you become incapacitated at some point while you are still alive. Having a plan in place can greatly reduce the stress of those responsibilities on your loved ones; it's just a loving thing to do.

We encourage our clients to use life insurance contracts to provide a legacy for their loved ones. We have several clients who have great pensions and Social Security, and really don't need their RMDs. We show them how to leverage those dollars to provide hundreds of thousands of dollars to leave to their children or charities. Life insurance benefits are free of income taxes, estate taxes, and inheritance taxes. Using a life insurance contract is one of the best ways to transition wealth in the United States.

Documents

There are a few documents that lay the groundwork of legacy planning. You've probably heard of all or most of them, but I'd like to review what they are and how people commonly use them. These are all things you should talk about with an estate planning attorney to establish your legacy.

Powers of Attorney

A power of attorney, or POA, is a document giving someone the authority to act on your behalf and in your best interests. These come in handy in situations where you cannot be present (think a vacation where you get stuck in Canada) or, for durable powers of attorney, even when you are incapacitated (think in a coma or coping with dementia).

It is important to have powers of attorney in place and to appoint someone you trust to act on your behalf in these matters. Have you ever heard of someone who was incapacitated after a car accident, whether from head trauma or being in a coma for weeks—sometimes months? Do you think their bills stopped coming due during that time? I like my phone company and my bank, but neither one is about to put a moratorium on sending me bills, particularly not for an extended or interminable period. A power of attorney would have the authority to pay your mortgage or cancel your cable while you are unable.

You can have multiple POAs and require them to act jointly.
What this looks like: Do you think two heads are better than one? One man, Chris, significantly relied on his two sons' opinions for both his business and personal matters. He appointed both sons as joint POA, requiring both their signoffs for his medical and financial matters.

You can have multiple POAs who can act independently.
What this looks like: Irene had three children with whom she routinely stayed. They lived in different areas of the country, which she thought was an advantage; one month she might be

hiking out West, the next she could enjoy the newest off-Broadway production, and the next she could soak up some Southern sun. She named her three children as independently authorized POAs, so, if something happened, no matter where she was, the child closest could step in to act on her behalf.

You can have POAs who have different responsibilities.
What this looks like: Although Luke's friend Claire, a nurse, was his go-to and POA for health-related issues, financial matters usually made her nervous, so he appointed his good neighbor, Matt, as his POA in all of his financial and legal matters.

In addition to POAs, it may be helpful to have an advanced medical directive. This is a document where you have pre-decided what choices you would make about different health scenarios. An advanced medical directive can help ease the burden for your medical POA and loved ones, particularly when it comes to end-of-life care.

We recommend that all seniors have POAs because at some point we are going to need help from either our children or a loved one we trust to act in our best interest. Financial institutions will not take any instructions unless the person provides a POA. We've seen cases where attorneys have gone before a judge to grant POA powers after a parent got sick or injured (or couldn't act on their own behalf). That doesn't work! We think the power Of attorney is one of the most important documents you can have.

Wills

Perhaps the most basic document of legacy planning, a will is a legal document wherein you outline your wishes for your estate. When it comes to your estate after your death, having a will is the foundation of your legacy. Without one, your loved ones are left behind, guessing what you would have wanted, and the court will likely split your assets according to the state's defaults. Maybe that's exactly what you wanted, as far as anyone knows, right? Because even if you told your nephew he could have your car he's been driving, if it's not in writing, it still might go to the brother, sister, son, or daughter to whom you aren't speaking.

However, it may not be enough just to have a will. Even with a will, your assets will be subject to probate. Probate is what we call the state's process for determining a will's validity. A judge will go through your will to question if it conflicts with state law, if it is the most up-to-date document, if you were mentally competent at the time it was in order, etc. For some, this is a quick, easily-resolved process. For others, particularly if someone steps forward to contest the will, it may take years to settle, all the while subjecting the assets to court costs and attorney's fees.

One other undesirable piece of the probate process is that it is a public process. That means anyone can go to the courthouse, ask for copies of the case, and discover your assets. They can also see who is slated to receive what and who is disputing.

Soul icon Aretha Franklin died without a will, for instance, and left a lot of money for people to fight over. And fight they did, in a harsh and very-public way.[40]

It's also important to remember beneficiary lines trump wills. So, that large life insurance policy? What if, when you bought it fifteen years ago, you wrote your ex-husband's name on the beneficiary line? Even if you stipulate otherwise in your will, the company that holds your policy will pay out to your ex-spouse. Or, how about the thousands of dollars in your IRA you dedicated to the children thirty years ago, but one of your

---

[40] Shane Jasmine Young. Young Law Group. May 3, 2021. "Almost Three Years After Her Death, Aretha Franklin's Poor Estate Planning Continues To Haunt Her Family." https://younglawnv.com/almost-three-years-after-her-death-aretha-franklins-poor-estate-planning-continues-to-haunt-her-family-part-1/

children was killed in a car accident, leaving his wife and two toddlers behind? That IRA is going to transfer to your remaining children, with nothing for your daughter-in-law and grandchildren.

That may paint a grim portrait, but I can't underscore enough the importance of working with a skilled estate planning attorney to keep your will and beneficiary lines up to date as your life changes, for the sake of your loved ones.

When I was growing up, I had a friend next door named Larry. Larry worked a long career for an electric company, and ended up divorcing and remarrying. He and his second wife had been married for twenty years, and raising kids and stepchildren, when Larry was diagnosed with cancer and died shortly thereafter.

In Pennsylvania, if you die without establishing a will, the state has one for you—and it isn't what you likely would have wanted. This is what happened to Larry and his family. His wife and kids weren't taken care of the way Larry would've wanted, all because he died without a will.

Trusts

Another piece of legacy planning to consider is the trust.

A trust is set up through an attorney and allows a third party, or trustee, to hold your assets and determine how they will pass to your beneficiaries. Many people are skeptical of trusts because they assume trusts are only appropriate for the fabulously wealthy.

However, a simple trust may only cost $1,000 to $2,500 in attorney's fees and can avoid both the expense and publicity of probate, provide a more immediate transfer of wealth, avoid some taxes, and provide you greater control over your legacy.[41]

For instance, if you want to set aside some funds for a grandchild's college education, you can make it a requirement he or she enrolls in classes before your trust will dispense any funds. Like a will, beneficiary lines will override your trust conditions, so you must still keep insurance policies and other assets up to date.

Like any financial or legal consideration, there are many options these days beyond the simple "yes or no" question of whether to have a trust. For one thing, you will need to consider if you want your trust to be revocable (you can change the terms while you are alive) or irrevocable (can't be changed; you are no longer the "owner" of the contents). A brief note here about irrevocable trusts: Although they have significant and greater tax benefits, they are still subject to a Medicaid look-back period. This means, if you transfer your assets into an irrevocable trust in an attempt to shelter them from a Medicaid spend-down, you will be ineligible for Medicaid coverage of long-term care for five years. Yet, an irrevocable trust can avoid both probate and estate taxes, and it can even protect assets from legal judgments against you.

Another thing to remember when it comes to trusts, in general, is, even if you have set up a trust, you must remember to fund it. In my three decades in practice, I've had numerous clients come to me, assuming they have protected their assets with a trust. When we talk about taxes and other pieces of their legacy, it turns out they never retitled any assets or changed any paperwork on the assets they wanted in the trust. So, please remember, a trust is just a bunch of fancy legal papers if you haven't followed through on retitling your assets.

---

[41] Regan Rondinelli-Haberek. LegalZoom. "What is the Average Cost to Prepare a Living Trust?" https://info.legalzoom.com/average-cost-prepare-living-trust-26932.html

Taxes

Although charitable contributions, trusts, and other tax-efficient strategies can reduce your tax bill, it's unlikely your estate will be passed on entirely tax-free. Yet, when it comes to building a legacy that can last for generations, taxes can be one of the heaviest drains on the impact of your hard work.

For 2017, the federal estate exemption was $5.49 million per individual and $10.98 million for a married couple, with estates facing up to a 40 percent tax rate after that. In 2021, those limits increased to $11.7 million for individuals and $23.4 million for married couples, with the 40 percent top level gift and estate tax remaining the same. Currently, the new estate limits are set to increase with inflation until Jan. 1, 2026, when they will "sunset" back to the inflation-adjusted 2017 limits.[42] And that's not taking into account the various state regulations and taxes regarding estate and inheritance transfers.

One "frequent flyer" on the tax concern list: retirement accounts.

Your IRA or 401(k) can be a source of tax issues when you pass away. For one thing, taking funds from a sizeable account can trigger a large tax bill. However, if you leave the assets in the account, there are still required minimum distributions (RMDs), which will take effect even after you die. If you pass the account to your spouse, he or she can keep taking your RMDs as is, or your spouse can retitle the account in his or her name and receive RMDs based on his or her life expectancy. Remember, if you don't take your RMDs, the IRS will take up to 50 percent of whatever your required distribution was, plus you will still have to pay income taxes whenever you withdraw that money. Thanks to rules enacted in 2020, anyone who inherits your IRA, with few exceptions (your spouse, a

---

[42] Laura Sanders, Richard Rubin. The Wall Street Journal. April 8, 2021. "Estate and Gift Taxes 2020-2021: Here's What You Need to Know" https://www.wsj.com/articles/estate-and-gift-taxes-2020-2021-heres-what-you-need-to-know-11617908256

beneficiary less than ten years younger, or a disabled adult child, to name a few), will need to empty the account within ten years of your death.

Also—and this is a pretty big also—check with an attorney if you are considering putting your IRA or 401(k) in a trust. An improperly titled beneficiary form for the IRA could mean the difference of thousands of dollars in taxes. This is just one more reason to work with a financial professional, one who can strategically partner with an estate planning attorney to diligently check your decisions.

When legacy planning is done correctly, people have peace of mind knowing that the income they're going to get, or the money they're going to inherit, will be free of income, estate, and inheritance taxes.

CHAPTER 9

Long-Term Care Insurance

Elsewhere in this book, I've outlined the risks longevity poses to your financial health. In fact, you may be tired of hearing it at this point.

Even so, I'd still like to repeat one more time—in case you've forgotten—it's estimated *seven* out of every ten Americans who reach age sixty-five will need long-term care of some kind.[43] Let me ask, if you knew the car you were going to be riding in had a 70 percent chance of having an accident, would you wear your seatbelt?

I had a client—I'll call her "Nancy"—who came in to get her taxes done, and every year she filed a joint tax return. About the third year, I asked "Why don't I ever get to see your husband?" It turns out he'd had dementia (at age fifty), and because they'd purchased long term care insurance with a lifetime benefit, he'd been in a nursing home for thirteen years by the time I asked about him.

The bottom line is we need to do a better job of planning for the possibility of long-term care. A public poll of Americans recently revealed nearly three-fourths of the public (74 percent) favor having a government-administered health plan available to all Americans to compete with private health

---

[43] Diane Omdahl. Forbes. January 14, 2020. "Does Medicare Pay For Long-Term Care? Don't Make A Big Mistake"
https://www.forbes.com/sites/dianeomdahl/2020/01/14/does-medicare-pay-for-long-term-care-dont-make-a-big-mistake/#f30eee411f39

insurance plans.[44] However, if you think about the current problems plaguing government-run programs such as Social Security, Medicaid, and Medicare, I think it stands to reason, for the time being, we're probably on our own.

Elsewhere, I covered the various ways of preparing for our own possible long-term care costs, from self-funding to insurance riders. I'd like to take a moment to expand on what is one of the most comprehensive coverage options: long-term care insurance.

LTCI Basics

The long-term care insurance, or LTCI, space has had a bit of a shakeup in the past few years. Many insurers stopped offering LTCI, and the policies remaining are often more expensive. In addition, denials of LTCI applications have risen to the point almost one-third of those between sixty and sixty-five are rejected.[45]

Those may sound like negatives—who wants fewer options with greater expense? Yet, the other side of the coin is the insurers who are left in the LTCI space have experience and policies that have endured. LTCI may be more expensive for individuals, but that's because they can be more expensive for insurers and because overall long-term care is just plain expensive, period. It's important to understand LTCI carriers aren't just making money hand-over-fist with these products. Instead, the carriers who have stopped selling policies were likely carriers who had unrealistic prices and underperforming policies. Unfortunately, it looks like the

---

[44] Kaiser Family Foundation. October 16, 2020. "Public Opinion on Single-Payer, National Health Plans, and Expanding Access to Medicare Coverage." https://www.kff.org/slideshow/public-opinion-on-single-payer-national-health-plans-and-expanding-access-to-medicare-coverage/
[45] Alexander Sammon. The American Prospect. October 20, 2020. "The Collapse of Long-Term Care Insurance."
https://prospect.org/familycare/the-collapse-of-long-term-care-insurance/

current market might only get more expensive in the next few decades.[46]

While many criticize the use-it-or-lose-it nature of LTCI, it is reasonable to consider that homeowner's insurance, car insurance, term life insurance, and many other types of insurance work the same way. Yes, you are paying into a policy in the hopes you may never use it. But, if you must use it, it can provide value well beyond the actual dollars you have paid into it. With an average of 353,100 home fires every year for the 128.45 million households in the United States, you have *less than a half a percent chance* of experiencing a home fire in any given year.[47, 48] Most of us would still squirm at the thought of not having homeowner's or renter's insurance to cover fire damage, however. Paradoxically, even with the statistics from the U.S. Department of Health and Human Services estimating we each have a *70 percent chance* of needing long-term care, only 7 percent of Americans have LTCI.[49, 50]

To purchase LTCI, you have to complete an application that includes a medical questionnaire. Depending on your age and the insurance carrier, you may also need to complete a

---

[46] American Association for Long-Term Care Insurance. January 12, 2021. "2021 Long Term Care Insurance Price Index Released." https://www.aaltci.org/news/long-term-care-insurance-association-news/2021-long-term-care-insurance-price-index-released-for-age-55

[47] Marty Ahrens. National Fire Prevention Association. November 2020. "Home Structure Fires." https://www.nfpa.org/News-and-Research/Data-research-and-tools/Building-and-Life-Safety/Home-Structure-Fires

[48] Statista. 2021. "Number of households in the U.S. from 1960 to 2020 (in millions)." https://www.statista.com/statistics/183635/number-of-households-in-the-us/

[49] Diane Omdahl. Forbes. January 14, 2020. "Does Medicare Pay For Long-Term Care? Don't Make A Big Mistake" https://www.forbes.com/sites/dianeomdahl/2020/01/14/does-medicare-pay-for-long-term-care-dont-make-a-big-mistake/#f30eee411f39

[50] Alexander Sammon. The American Prospect. October 20, 2020. "The Collapse of Long-Term Care Insurance." https://prospect.org/familycare/the-collapse-of-long-term-care-insurance/

medical exam. If you qualify, then the insurance company will offer you a policy with certain coverage and pricing based in part on your odds of needing long-term care in the future. The younger you are, the more likely you are to qualify—at a rate that is more likely affordable for you.

LTCI premiums count as medical expenses and may potentially be paid with special tax considerations. For instance, if you are eligible to itemize your medical expenses, LTCI premiums can be itemized. Or, alternately, you can pay premiums with tax-free money in health savings accounts. The amount you can withdraw tax-free for LTCI premiums depends on your age.

If you have an LTCI policy, coverage will typically kick in when you have been medically shown to be unable to perform two or more activities of daily living (ADLs). An ADL is an activity such as bathing, toileting, eating, dressing, grooming, etc. These are all things we naturally prefer to do by ourselves; they are markers of our independence and ability to take care of ourselves. Once someone is unable to do some of these things alone, they need long-term help. So, if you have LTCI, once you reach this point you will qualify for a daily amount of coverage over a pre-selected time period, depending on the terms of your policy. That money could be used to cover a nursing home, in-home care, or community organization care. The benefits will begin after the policy's elimination period, which you choose when you purchase the policy. The elimination period can range from 0 to 180 days, and the shorter the elimination period, the higher the premium.

With LTCI, you can pick and choose facilities or care options according to your standards instead of having the government decide what is best for you.

Long-Term Care Partnership Program

One other significant advantage of LTCI is many plans are eligible for a federal-state government initiative called the

Long-Term Care Partnership Program.[51] This program is a joint effort by the federal government and certain states to help individuals decide to choose LTCI protection. It means, if you deplete your LTCI coverage and find yourself in a position of having to spend down your assets to become eligible for Medicaid, part or all of your LTCI coverage limit will extend to your assets. Here's what this might look like "in real life" (using, of course, a completely hypothetical person):

Jennifer chooses an LTCI policy to cover up to three years of nursing home care (a little more than the average long-term care stay) in a semi-private room. After several injuries render her unable to dress or bathe herself, Jennifer moves to Winters Retirement Community. Jennifer is not average. Her policy has paid out more than $250,000 on her behalf, and her policy benefits are now exhausted. This puts her in position for a Medicaid spend down before Medicaid will cover the cost of her long-term care. However, because she purchased a policy her state approved in line with the Long-Term Care Partnership Program, instead of having to spend down her assets to the Medicaid requirement and leaving very little for her family to inherit, she is allowed to set aside $250,000 on top of her state's other spend-down exemptions.

Remember "Nancy," from the previous example? She and her husband had the foresight to do it right—to provide for their long-term care *before* they knew what they'd need.

LTCI — It's Not Just About You

Aside from the aforementioned partnership program and possible tax advantages of traditional LTCI, I think perhaps one of the most compelling arguments in favor of preparing

---

[51] American Association for Long-Term Care Insurance. 2022. "Long Term Care Insurance Partnership Plans." http://www.aaltci.org/long-term-care-insurance/learning-center/long-term-care-insurance-partnership-plans.php

for the likelihood of long-term care has less to do with our own personal assets and more to do with others.

What do I mean? Well, I hear from lots of people who think it won't matter. "Oh, by the time I reach the point of needing long-term care, I'll be out of my mind. Who cares who takes care of me and how that happens?"

I even had a recent client who had a nest egg of two million dollars and no children to worry about. He told me that, when the time came, he'd just "drive down the road!" This was the "plan" he thought he had.

However, like estate planning, long-term care planning isn't solely about us. In fact, I might argue that the most important piece of long-term care planning isn't about you at all. It's about your loved ones. It's about your spouse, your children, or your friends, and how caring for you could impact them if you don't have the necessary resources.

Most caregiving happens in people's private homes. A survey of caregivers reveals just a sampling of how a long stint of caring for relatives and loved ones can affect the caregivers:[52]

- Of those surveyed, an average of nineteen hours a week was provided in care. Among those, about 38 percent had to cut back their hours at their job
- Caregivers missed an average of six hours per week at work
- More than 50 percent said their personal and mental health was impacted, including depression and a lower standard of living
- 66 percent of caregivers used their personal assets, like savings and retirement funds, to pay for a loved one's care

We offer LTCI because 70 percent of people are going to need it in their lifetime. Only 20 percent of us never need it—

---

[52] Genworth. November 16, 2021. "Beyond Dollars 2021."
https://pro.genworth.com/riiproweb/productinfo/pdf/682801BRO.pdf

usually because we die younger than we wanted to. But most will need long-term care, either at home or in a facility. When we explain that their children can be paid to care for them in their home, most people think that makes more sense for them than going into a facility. And that's just one example of how thinking through the probability of needing long-term care should be part of a true *Roadmap to Retirement.*

Because of its benefits for both the policy holder and his or her family or caregiver, LTCI can be a valuable asset in any retirement plan.

CHAPTER 10

Finding a Financial Professional

I was twenty-five when I got the call in the middle of the night—the kind of call nobody wants to get.

Grandpa Bill had died.

My parents married young—in their teen years—and I spent a great deal of time with my grandparents growing up. I'd been named after my grandfather, and we were very close.

I was sad to hear he'd passed away, of course, but what I came to learn about how his death affected my grandmother actually changed my life.

Grandpa Bill's death was unexpected. He was in his early sixties, and hadn't retired yet. As a consequence, my grandmother couldn't take advantage of the pension he'd worked his whole life to earn.

She had retired at sixty-two, and did have a Social Security check, but the couple had planned on a nice retirement, with two Social Security checks and a pension to last them through their golden years.

Upon Grandpa's death, Grandma was left with nothing but one Social Security check and some money they'd saved.

Her retirement was changed, and dramatically.

It was then I knew I had to be involved in helping seniors with their finances.

I started by doing tax preparation for seniors, and soon I was developing relationships and coming to understand that seniors have different needs from those of younger folks. I realized I wanted to specialize in helping people plan for a great retirement.

That's why I'm passionate about helping people create a *Roadmap to Retirement*. When you have that roadmap, it ensures that you won't get off the road to the golden years you envision, no matter what happens.

***

In our firm, we practice *safe money* retirement planning. What that means to us is that the *Roadmap to Retirement* we create with our clients ensures that they can't lose any of their money once they're relying on their retirement nest egg.

For some firms, "safe money" means they'll make sure you won't lose more than 30 percent of your retirement money.

To us, that isn't really "safe" money.

Whether they're our clients or not, we hope folks will find their way to this safe money retirement. For that reason, we strongly urge people not to "DIY"—do it yourself—but to seek the help of a qualified financial advisor. Ideally, you'll want advice from a professional who realizes that seniors are not in a position to lose *any* of their hard-earned retirement money.

I've worked hard to earn the kind of credentials seniors can trust when it comes to working with a retirement advisor. I've served in the industry for nearly thirty years, I'm a Life Underwriter Training Council Fellow (LUTCF) and a registered financial consultant.

And, as a true fiduciary, I'm committed to working in the best interest of my clients, without distraction. Unlike some firms which offer only certain financial products, my firm scans the universe of instruments to find what's most appropriate for our clients in every case.

***

There are many other reasons folks should seek the help of a qualified financial advisor when it's time to retire:

- A qualified professional understands the industry terms, such as "required minimum distribution," and can help cut through the jargon to make things understandable for clients
- A qualified advisor knows the tax laws that affect seniors in retirement, and keeps up-to-date on the rapid changes in the relevant tax code
- A qualified pro has the experience to advise clients across a wide spectrum of issues that specifically affect seniors, such as inflation, health care, and the special needs of a person who's lost their spouse.

Unless a person has studied the intricacies of these issues, and gained experience working with retirees from all walks of life, they aren't really qualified to advise seniors who need financial guidance.

Those seniors need a true guide, like the *Roadmap to Retirement* my firm has worked hard to become qualified to provide.

***

Retirement today is completely different from what it was "back in the day."

People retiring these days don't have the sort of pensions upon which their parents and grandparents would have relied—plans into which their employers contributed most or all of the funds, and which grew with interest to create nest eggs for their retired employees.

These pension plans have been replaced by 401(k) and 403(b) plans, which require employees to elect to save money from their paychecks which their employers then match to create a growing retirement fund.

As such, these new instruments don't provide the same kinds of guarantees (let alone gold watches) that came with the old-fashioned pension plan.

This makes DIY retirement planning all the more tempting. After all, many people like to feel they're "in control" of their choices in terms of how much to put aside and where to invest the money.

It also makes seeking a truly qualified retirement advisor much more important than it would have been for pensioners of a generation or two ago.

It's also important to find someone you can *trust*, and with whom you can relate. A qualified advisor will know their stuff, but you'd also want someone who's in a position to understand your unique circumstances as a person, as a couple, and as a family.

I love to work with seniors, and hear the stories that make their situations unique. And I don't mind sharing my own stories, like the one about my grandparents with which I started this chapter. That's how people connect, and it's my passion to find that connection with my clients. It makes helping them plan for their golden years so much easier (and more effective).

There isn't just one *Roadmap to Retirement* that we can take off the shelf and offer every person or couple we meet. Each *Roadmap* has to start where you are, and lead where you want to go, given the "landscape" of your unique story.

***

How do you find the right advisor?

First, never discount the power of *word of mouth*. Many of our clients came to our firm because they'd heard about us from friends, neighbors, or members of their family. So your first step in finding the right advisor for you might well be to talk to the people you know who've had experience with a financial advisor.

You want to learn about a *specialist* in retirement planning. In our firm, we only work with folks fifty and older—we're true retirement specialists. Another advisor might be extremely smart and effective, but if they don't specialize in retirement, they probably won't be up-to-speed on the issues that specifically affect seniors and folks looking to enjoy their best retirement.

Taxation matters are key for retirees. So when you're looking for a qualified retirement advisor, try to find someone who's well versed in taxes, and who makes a point of staying abreast of the ever-changing rules and procedures regarding taxation.

When you meet with a "candidate" advisor, it won't take long before you'll know if they're a trustworthy specialist who has the experience and expertise to guide you through the issues that matter most to you.

Meanwhile, be on the lookout for "red flags" that indicate that you might want to continue the search.

When an advisor seems to be "pushing" financial products they tell you earn a very high rate of return, it's tempting to agree to their advice and invest in their products. But beware: with high return comes high risk. Can you really afford to lose a substantial amount of your hard-earned retirement nest egg, especially once your paychecks come to an end? Most seniors understand they no longer have time to recover their savings from a significant loss.

A newer advisor is not likely to be a good fit for seniors. If an advisor has been in business less than a year, for instance, they won't have had time to learn and experience the things a truly qualified professional needs to know in order to create a true *Roadmap* to your unique retirement.

Finally, trust your gut. If you don't get a good feeling talking with an advisor—if they don't relate well with you or seem to "get" you and your situation—keep looking.

***

You might find more than one advisor who specializes in issues unique to seniors, and who understands the ins and outs of taxation, liquidity, inflation, health care, and so forth.

If you find more than one advisor who's qualified in terms of knowledge and experience, choose the one you most feel you can trust. Often, that's the advisor who's willing to have the hard conversations that are sometimes necessary, without harming the collegial relationship.

For instance, I've worked with more than one couple who had the sort of arrangement that was very typical a generation or two ago: The husband worked a long career to earn a pension, while the wife took care of the home and family.

The hard conversation sometimes arises when the career spouse (the husband, in most of those cases) had made certain elections with his pension plan which didn't account for the eventuality of his own passing.

Most of those pension plans allowed the employee to choose how much they would take in monthly distributions, and if they didn't take the maximum, they could leave a portion for the surviving spouse after their own death.

I've made a specialty out of having these tough talks, only to make sure both spouses fully understand the true consequences of choices that may have been made years ago. It's never too late: With the right *Roadmap*, the couple can start putting some of their larger pension payments into safe money instruments that can provide for the surviving spouse upon death of the pensioner.

We can have these difficult conversations without alienating people or making anyone feel foolish. But that's the kind of skill that only comes with decades of experience with seniors in all kinds of situations.

Your best bet is to find an advisor who's on top of all the substantive issues, but with whom you can talk as you would with a true friend—someone who always has the best interests of everyone in your family at heart.

***

I like to start working with people when they're around fifty years of age, so that there's time to build a truly wonderful nest egg for their golden years. But whenever they come to see me, and no matter whether they want to retire at sixty-two or seventy (or at any other point), I do whatever's necessary to create a true *Roadmap to Retirement* for my clients.

Having a *Roadmap to Retirement* means my clients can rest easy, knowing they have income they can rely on for the rest of their lives, no matter what happens.

After many years of working with seniors, I've come to learn that almost all of them have one thing on the top of their minds: They want to know they're "going to be okay."

For that reason, I've focused my practice on making sure I can tell folks that they *will* be okay on the road through their golden years, no matter what bumps in the road they encounter.

I wonder if Grandma stayed awake at night, worrying about the future, after Grandpa Bill died. I'll bet she did. And it makes me sad to think so.

I wouldn't have wanted my grandmother to spend sleepless nights worrying about her future, and I don't know anyone who'd want to leave their loved ones in that situation. I strive, all the time, to treat my clients like family, and to give them the peace of mind they need to sleep well at night.

That's the kind of sleep you get when you have a true *Roadmap to Retirement*.

Acknowledgments

I'd like to thank Michael Patrick, Sr., the father of my high school best friend, for providing the guidance and inspiration necessary to my career—and to the writing of this book. As an insurance professional, he brought me into his practice and taught me a great deal about integrity, hard work, and earning people's trust. He was a valued member of the community, and was seen as a force for good in helping improve people's lives. I thank him for his mentorship, without which this book (and my career) would not have been possible.

I'd also like to acknowledge the hard work and dedication of my staff at Ilgenfritz Financial Group, and in particular, Kate and Mel, whose help has been instrumental in pulling together the content of this book.

Finally, I can't close without thanking my family for their love and support, and particularly my dad. Dad was always in my corner, teaching me the value of hard work, and inspiring me to believe anything is achievable if you're willing to earn it.

WILLIAM ILGENFRITZ
About the Author

William Ilgenfritz

As the founder of Ilgenfritz Financial Group, William Ilgenfritz is focused on helping clients work toward their retirement dreams through a well-thought-out strategy for retirement income.

William got his start in the industry in 1993, as a life insurance agent with New England Financial. Since then, he's developed the *Roadmap to Retirement* as an integral part of the senior-focused practice of his firm. He truly enjoys helping seniors dream big and plan well for a great retirement.

William holds life and health licenses in Pennsylvania and Maryland, and earned his Life Underwriter Training Council Fellow (LUTCF) designation nearly three decades ago. He has a Bachelor of Science degree in finance from West Virginia University.

Printed in China